TAKE A GIRL LIKE ME

TAKE A GIRL LIKE ME

Life With George

DIANA MELLY

Published by Chatto & Windus 2005

2 4 6 8 10 9 7 5 3 1

Copyright © Diana Melly 2005

Diana Melly has asserted her right under the Copyright, Designs and Patents Act 1988 to
be identified as the author of this work

First published in Great Britain in 2005 by
Chatto & Windus
Random House, 20 Vauxhall Bridge Road,
London SW1V 2SA

Random House Australia (Pty) Limited
20 Alfred Street, Milsons Point, Sydney,
New South Wales 2061, Australia

Random House New Zealand Limited
18 Poland Road, Glenfield,
Auckland 10, New Zealand

Random House (Pty) Limited
Endulini, 5A Jubilee Road, Parktown 2193, South Africa

The Random House Group Limited Reg. No. 954009
www.randomhouse.co.uk

A CIP catalogue record for this book is available from the British Library

ISBN 0 7011 7906 6

Papers used by The Random House Group Limited are natural, recyclable products made
from wood grown in sustainable forests; the manufacturing processes conform to the
environmental regulations of the country of origin

Typeset by SX Composing DTP, Rayleigh, Essex
Printed and bound in Great Britain by
Clays Ltd, St Ives Plc

FOR CARMEN, KEZZIE AND GEORGE

A simple crude fellow is a character fit to bear true witness; for clever people observe more things and more curiously, but they interpret them; and to lend weight and conviction to their interpretation, they cannot help altering history a little. They never show you things as they are, but bend and disguise them according to the way they have seen them; and to give credence to their judgment and attract you to it, they are prone to add something to their matter, to stretch it out and amplify it. We need a man either very honest, or so simple that he has not the stuff to build up false inventions and give them plausibility.

Montaigne, 'On Cannibals'

Contents

CHAPTER I

A Winter's Tale

In 1961 when I met George I was twenty-four and married to my second husband. I had two children, Patrick who was six and Candy who was seven months. Some people thought I was beautiful, but not everyone. I had once been a model and when a famous photographer tried me out, he told a fashion editor, 'No matter what I do with her, she just looks like a little old lady.'

George was thirty-five, quite short and just getting to be rather plump; his feet were tiny so he minced slightly when he walked; he had brown eyes, a big nose, a huge smile and was famous for singing in a jazz band and being bisexual.

There is a side to George that has always been attracted to unstable, needy women – and that was me. I responded to almost any man who wanted me. Until I met George, this haphazard selection usually ended unhappily.

When I married Michael, my first husband, I was sixteen. He was an imaginative, feckless Irishman of aristocratic origins which impressed me at the time but meant that he considered most jobs beneath him. We lived in bed-sits on hand-outs from my mother who was working as a housekeeper. Debt collectors came round most mornings. One of them, who came with a writ from the gas board, ignored the fact that I was eight months pregnant and made a heavy pass at me. 'Don't worry girlie,' he had said, 'I could sort this out for you if you're nice to me.'

When our son Patrick was seven months old, Michael was still out of work. Unable to afford the rent of a flat or even a room, we went to live with his parents in Sussex. My mother-in-law and I disliked each other and after a few weeks I walked out, left Michael and, taking Patrick with me, went home to my mother. Her employer only allowed us to stay for a couple of months, saying that I should stand on my own two feet.

I found a room, I waitressed at night and was moderately successful at modelling. During the day Patrick went to a crèche, at night he was left alone. Sometimes after leaving the coffee bar where I worked I went out dancing. Then Patrick got measles and I had to stop work. The money ran out and I sent Patrick, now two, to live with my aunt in Essex. After leaving Patrick, I went to live with a writer called Michael Alexander who took me to Afghanistan. We travelled there in his battered Land Rover while he gathered material for a book.

When we came back, he left me and married someone else. I got 'engaged' to three different men. None of them seemed too desolate when I changed my mind except for one. Johnnie Moynihan was a journalist, we had the same friends, he was kind to his mother and I ran out of reasons for saying no.

But it was another year before Patrick came to live with us, because Johnnie wanted to wait until we had a child of our own. So when my aunt brought Patrick to the London flat, our daughter Candy was already three months old. Just six weeks later Johnnie was sent to Paris by his paper, the *Evening Standard*. The job was to last for two months and he was lent a large flat near Les Deux Magots on the left bank. I went too but we left the children behind: Candy with my mother and Patrick back with my aunt. Johnnie had given two reasons for not wanting the children to come: money, and the busy social life that we would have to lead. I missed them and, when Johnnie heard that he was being sent down to Monte Carlo for a further month, I decided to go home.

We had let our flat for the duration of the French assignment, so after visiting Patrick at my aunt's house, I squashed into my mother's tiny bed-sit with Candy, who at six months was still just small enough for a carry-cot. Five years before, when I'd run away from Michael taking Patrick with me, my mother and I had shared the same bed. Patrick had slept on two chairs tied together because I couldn't afford a cot.

Back there again, I still didn't like staying at home with my mother. I would often leave her to babysit and would climb the rather grubby stairs to Muriel's, a drinking club in Soho. Encouraged by Muriel, someone would usually buy me a drink and I would go and sit with it on top of the piano. I always imagined that my rather short legs would look better if I was high up. One night George came in and everyone perked up. He came over to me, and then said to Muriel, 'Who's the sexy mouse?' For some reason young women were called mice in the days before they were called birds. 'That's Johnnie Moynihan's wife,' said Muriel, looking pleased. Any possible sexual encounter involving trouble always excited her.

I knew that George Melly was well known in a small circle of jazz fans and to habitués of Soho. I also knew that he wrote a strip cartoon for the *Daily Mail* and I had seen him on a news programme talking about the nuclear threat and wearing a ban-the-bomb badge. He had a reputation for being sexually wild and a boozer. There was a buzz when he was expected, either on a left-wing march or at a Chelsea bottle party. He had given me such a big hug at one of those parties that my breast milk (I was feeding Candy at the time) had soaked through the pads in my bra. At another party I was talking to his wife Victoria and another woman, both of them models. George swayed up to us and said he didn't know which of us was the more beautiful, or whom he should give the apple to. Once I arrived at a party in a studio in Paddington just too late to see him being carried off by a huge West Indian belly dancer. It was rumoured that she had first knocked him out.

George was flirting with me in Muriel's when the phone rang. It was his wife, Victoria, explaining that she couldn't meet him that evening to go to the opening of the Establishment Club. The idea for the club, a place where you could have supper and watch a satirical cabaret, came from Peter Cook and Dudley Moore. It had attracted a huge amount of publicity and invitations for the opening were in demand. Naturally I accepted when George invited me to take Victoria's place. Later on that evening George and I made love on Hampstead Heath.

The following day we met in a pub and rather casually decided that somehow we would live together. Victoria had recently agreed to move in with Roy Boulting, the film director, but Johnnie was angry and hurt. Coldly I ignored his feelings and, taking the children, moved into Andrée Melly's flat. George's sister was an actress and was away rehearsing in Bristol, but she sent George a firm letter: yes, I could stay there until Victoria moved out, but Tizzy, their brother Bill's girlfriend, was also staying there and she was more conventional. The letter laid out the rules:

1. Not to let Tizzy be a penny out of pocket *re* food
2. Not to get tight and use bad language
3. Not to fuck in the flat
4. To be charming to Tizzy's mother.

Two weeks later I moved into George's house on the borders of Golders Green and Hampstead. He was singing three or four times a week with Mick Mulligan's band, and that night was on tour in the North. Victoria had moved out only that day. She had taken her child Pandora, her sports car, the brass cot from Harrods and the portrait of herself painted by Tim Whidborne, who she said was the father of her child. (Tim was a pupil of Annigoni, who painted the famous portrait of the Queen.) George rang me from the Manchester Jazz Club and asked me to hang 'the lamb painting' in place of her portrait above the mantelpiece. George had bought paintings since his father had given him £200 when he was eighteen. He was now thirty-five and it was a large collection: Magritte, Max Ernst, Picasso and others less well known. I searched the house for a lamb in any shape or form – Cubist, Surrealist, Kitsch. No lamb, and nothing signed Lamb.

I knew better than to own up to this hole in my knowledge of art. The previous week I had gone to a jazz club with George and had been asked to find 'Bix', the piano player. I found a man practising some chords on the piano and asked him if his name was 'Bix'. I hadn't heard of Bix Beiderbecke, the famous American jazz musician, and when Ronnie – for that was his real name – told the band of my ignorance they had a good laugh at my expense. They also enjoyed it when I clapped on the on-beat.

The only member of the band that I got on well with was Mick Mulligan, the band-leader. He was a tall, shambling man, good-looking with a strong sexual aura softened by a fatherly manner. Perhaps I also liked him because he said to

George, on meeting me for the first time, 'You've got a good one there, cock.' I also liked Ian Christie, the clarinettist who became a film critic for the *Daily Express* when the band folded; but Ian thought I was a snob and didn't have much to say to me. The rest of the band didn't think my reign would last long and treated me accordingly.

When George came back from Manchester he asked me why I hadn't hung the lamb and I replied I had tried it and it hadn't looked good. It was some months before I spotted 'the lamb'. It was Wilfredo Lam, not a terrifically well-known painter, with an indecipherable signature.

In 1960, the year before I met George, there had been a demonstration against nuclear weapons culminating in a big sit-down in Trafalgar Square. I watched it on the TV and had seen George being carried off by the police along with Vanessa Redgrave, John Osborne and Doris Lessing. He always wore his ban-the-bomb badge, and once, when he was asked to remove it for a TV programme about trad jazz, he refused and his song was cut from the show.

Not all of his defiant gestures were equally attractive. I always disliked the point system. While travelling in the bandwagon, the Mulligan band would award themselves points whenever they had the opportunity to run over a disabled person. It was six points for a blind man and eight if he was also on crutches, and the same for a pregnant woman. But these were the days before political correctness, when de Sade was only seen as a great liberator. It was also before feminism and the British jazz world was as full of male chauvinists as other more conventional worlds. Men knew best and I never corrected them.

CHAPTER 2

A Jazz Musician in Prosperous Circumstances

George's house was in a cul-de-sac that led on to Hampstead Heath. In the nineteenth century it had been a washerwoman's cottage and the deeds gave us permission to hang washing on the Heath and tether a goat there.

I immediately settled in properly by getting ill with bronchitis. George's sister Andrée came to see me when she was back from tour. She had taken on the task of telling Maudie, George's mother, the tale of the new woman in her eldest son's life, who had already been married twice and had two children. Maudie sent me a very long and chatty letter when she heard I was ill. We finally met on Victoria station, supposedly neutral territory. Maudie wrote to George saying I was 'very sweet', not at all what she had imagined, although she wasn't sure about black stockings worn with pink shoes.

The first time I went to Liverpool I was nervous. George

was in love with his native city, and there was Maudie to meet, as well as all the girlfriends. They had been heavily romanticised by George: Lucy the flower-seller's daughter, Mary a performance artist. They were both very fey and looked like the girls in pre-Raphaelite paintings. At the Cavern where George was performing they came to inspect me; word had got round that, surprisingly, George now had a permanent partner.

Back in Maudie's huge rambling Victorian house I questioned him thoroughly about them: how long had he gone out with Lucy, did she stay all night, did he do this with her, and did she do that to him. Perhaps he liked the attention, or thought it was proof of how passionately in love with him I was – and I was – but it must have been tiring.

We slept in what had been the room George shared with his brother Bill. George warned me that Maudie would wait twenty minutes after we'd gone up and then enter the bedroom with some excuse. I climbed into his bed and, just as we started to make love, Maudie entered carrying a long stick. This turned out to be a pole with a hook on the end. She marched across the floor, hooked the pole on to the window latch and opened it a couple of inches. She then left, saying, 'I shouldn't have thought that bed was big enough for both of you. What do you want for breakfast? When am I going to meet your mother?'

She also wanted to meet my children, Patrick and Candy. Maudie had adored Victoria's child Pandora, and before my arrival had not been told that there was any doubt about Pandora's paternity. Again it was Andrée who had the task of giving Maudie some rough news: George was not Pandora's father and therefore Maudie had lost her grandchild. It was very hard on her, but she was a kind, fair woman and she made a huge effort with my two. George had nicknamed Candy 'Miss Jolly Grin Grin' but Patrick he nicknamed 'Grunt'. Patrick had been accepted at the local primary school and also at a child guidance clinic in Camden Town. There, a kind woman, whom Patrick called 'Miss Horrible, Horrible', attempted to undo some of the harm that he had suffered.

Patrick was six years old when he came to live with Johnnie and me; now, five months later, he was presented with another new father, a new home and a new school. But he was clever and his life had made him independent beyond his years. He was also popular with other children and extremely rebellious.

For Candy things were different. Apart from the four weeks I had spent in Paris, I had always been there and, although Johnnie loved his daughter, this was before the days when fathers cuddled their babies or changed nappies. Once a week my mother would spend the day at our house while George and I went to the pub so that Johnnie could come and look at his daughter for a couple of hours. Our behaviour was unbelievably selfish and heartless, we never avoided places like Muriel's where we might bump into him and we flaunted our romance wherever we went. It seemed as if we were drunk with sex and could never get enough of each other. One night while George was introducing me to the dubious pleasures of a 'knee tremble' in a dimly lit alley way, we became aware that a policeman was silently watching us. Hurriedly we adjusted our clothing and moved off. That was before my divorce and, had we been arrested, it might have jeopardised my getting custody of the children.

George was away singing with Mick Mulligan's band two or three days a week and I was terrified to let him go alone. I'd now been to enough gigs with him to know that the temptations of the willing 'scrubbers', as the female available fans were called, could be irresistible, particularly if they had red hair.

We engaged an au pair so that I could travel with him. First there was Florence, an art student from Paris who didn't like to start her day before eleven a.m. Then we found Betty who was sixteen and had been in care since she was four. Betty developed a huge crush on me: she would give me sloppy wet kisses as near to my mouth as she could get. She hated George and once took Patrick and Candy out on a boat. None of them could swim.

We 'let Betty go' and my mother volunteered to be our next au pair and left her housekeeping job. Because I was so practical, my mother started using the nickname that had originated when we had lived together: 'Miss Perfect', she used to call me in those days, because it was always I who remembered to make sure that we had coins for the gas meter, told her off if her hem was coming down, fixed the lights if they fused and called the doctor when she got her twice-yearly bronchitis; at fifteen I was already very bossy. George loved the name and when he drew cartoons of me, would always put a halo above my head.

I was now pregnant with Tom and pleased not to have the responsibility of the two children. I thought I needed to be with George. Maudie bought us a little green minivan, Andrée gave me driving practice and I passed my test with just three weeks of lessons. Now I could drive George not just to gigs but to the BBC if he was doing a programme, or to Fleet Street. The *Daily Mail* published a strip cartoon called *Flook*, for which George wrote the balloons and Wally Fawkes drew the pictures; they met every month with the editor. Most of the national papers were in Fleet Street then and, as there were no parking restrictions, I would wait for him in the car just to make sure he didn't get off with a secretary.

I'd never been to the Midlands or the North of England before I travelled with George and I loved the novelty of staying in artists' digs or sleeping in the back of the van. Once, having parked in a seemingly empty field, we woke to find the van swaying from side to side as a herd of cows rubbed themselves against us. We lay there for an hour waiting for the farmer to rescue us, drinking the coffee from a Thermos flask that 'Mrs Perfect' always remembered to take. In Swansea we stayed with Kingsley Amis. In the morning we made love in a bed that was propped up on one side with old paperbacks. Amis came in and retreated, apologising politely.

Going to jazz clubs, being one of the favoured few who didn't have to queue or pay to get in, was thrilling. But the best part was standing near the front of the enraptured crowd knowing that I was the envy of the other girls. In 'There'll be some Changes Made' George would point at me as he sang about changing his 'long, tall thin one' for a 'little short fat one'. I was shorter than Victoria, and, once pregnant with Tom, certainly fatter. In 'Mack the Knife' George sang about Sukie Tawdry, Lotte Lenya, and sweet Georgia Brown, pointing at different girls in turn, but I was always 'Sweet Georgia Brown' and his finger rested on me the longest.

Every year George sang at the Anarchists' Ball and in 1963 it coincided with the night that Hugh Gaitskell died. Gaitskell had been the leader of the Labour party since 1955 when Clement Attlee resigned; he was considered to be an honest politician and a man of integrity. He was also a very social animal; once I was specially invited to a dinner party because he liked to dance and needed a partner. We danced sedately round the room and I remembered him as being very funny and kind. It was a shock to hear his death being celebrated by an anarchist, who got up on stage and said, 'The only good politician is a dead one.'

As long as I could squeeze behind the wheel, I was determined to go on tour too. We wanted to get married before the birth but were waiting for both our divorces to be finalised. John Mortimer was my lawyer and when the judge asked him if the children would be well cared for, Mortimer replied, 'Mr Melly is a jazz musician in prosperous circum-stances.' And because I was so obviously very pregnant the judge waived the necessity of waiting the traditional three months for the decree nisi.

On the day of the wedding I had just driven back from Edinburgh, and since the baby was almost due, on the way to the register office we picked up the box of sterilised equipment needed for a home delivery. Outside the office was a taxi rank and when we came out the second taxi in the line was white. It was unusual for taxis to be anything other than black so George went up to the driver of the first one and, explaining that we had just got married, asked if he minded if we took the white one. 'About bloody time,' was all the reply he got. We went to the Ivy for a celebratory lunch, but I threw up in the Ladies and had to be taken home. Forty-eight hours later Tom was born.

He was a month early, and when I woke at five a.m. knowing I was in labour I rang for the midwife to come. She suggested that I ring back in a few hours, but an hour later George was delivering Tom and the midwife only arrived in time to cut the cord and wash him. George was thrilled, not only with Tom but because the midwife was a nun and had washed her hands under Magritte's painting *Le Viol*. Victoria hadn't allowed him to hang this painting, and Maudie used to ask him if he was famous enough to own it. The painting is of a woman's face, but instead of eyes, nose and mouth, she has breasts, a navel and a vagina.

I thought nothing would stop me going on tour, but once, in the middle of a five-day tour, I got a call from my mother saying that Candy had bronchitis and the doctor had told her to send for me. I left at once and drove back from Birmingham sick with anxiety, not just for Candy but because I'd seen an attractive redhead eyeing George. A few days later I got ill and then my mother did too. The doctor came and said that she should go to bed and I should get up.

My mother had often been ill when I was growing up; I hated nursing her then and I hated it now. It also meant that even with Candy better, I couldn't go on tour with George and I was full of adolescent fear and rage. From that moment it was obvious that our arrangement wasn't working and she decided to go back to her old job. We had not always been kind to her: George had mocked her sad attempts to be clever or witty and often imitated her. She had blue eyes of which she was very proud and she was also tiny. She was not allowed to think that either of these physical attributes were anything but laughable and George would say 'I'm looking over a four-leaf clover – but only just' and then he would flutter his eyes. She was keen on quotations and had a slight lisp; she would say, 'A wose is a wose is a wose,' but no matter how much she was teased she was always maddeningly cheerful.

After she'd gone we decided to engage a mother's help with a child of her own. Our reasons, as always, were selfish: she wouldn't want to go out much, and being a mother herself wouldn't need mothering by me. Dorothy wasn't Welsh, but she had been working in a children's home in South Wales and the father of her child was Welsh. She affected a strong Welsh accent. Dorothy and Baby Jim came to us when Jim was six weeks old and Tom was five months. Dorothy's stories of the humiliations of the 'unmarried mothers' home' filled us with satisfactory indignation; not so much the endless floor scrubbing, but the girls and their bulges being paraded through the streets on their obligatory way to church every Sunday.

During those first three or four years we lived in a haze of irritating-to-others, uxorious bliss. Leaving the children with the various helps we spent our days in Muriel's club and Wheeler's restaurant. Both of these establishments were patronised by bohemian London. Francis Bacon was a glamorous and regular customer. One afternoon he stopped us as we were leaving the club and after embracing George, he poked a finger at me and drawled, 'I've never quite seen the point of you.'

I inhaled as many of George's interests as I could. Never again would I make the Bix Beiderbecke mistake. I knew every Ma Rainie song and every detail of Bessie Smith's turbulent life. I preferred Chicago blues to Louis Armstrong but secretly admired Helen Shapiro and Adam Faith. My knowledge of pop music eventually became useful to George when he was asked to write a column for the *Observer*.

Surrealism was easy to mug up and I crammed books about Dada, Miró, Magritte and Ernst. Some of the latter we had hanging on the walls. I read *Nadja* by André Breton, and his portrait of the heroine made me realise just how much George liked mad, difficult women. It was his favourite book.

I didn't need to be taught about books; since I was eighteen I had read a lot and met a few writers and publishers. Through Michael Alexander, the man I had gone to Afghanistan with, I had met the publisher George Weidenfeld. It was one evening, when the three of us were having supper, that Weidenfeld had suggested Michael should write a book about a journey through Turkey and Iran to Afghanistan and take me with him. That was how I came to have my twenty-first birthday in an Afghan valley.

Weidenfeld and I had remained friends and, when I introduced him to George, he invited him to write a book about the jazz world. Weidenfeld was famous, not only for being irresistible to women and inviting everyone he knew to write a book, but also for his parties. Before it was published, George's book, *Owning Up*, had received an excellent reader's report and we heard that at least two important critics liked it a lot. We assumed that Weidenfeld would give us one of his famous parties, but, perhaps imagining that the jazz musicians and the scrubbers who might be invited would not look well in his drawing-room, he gave us £50 and suggested we host it ourselves.

Fishing was an obsession of George's, which I never took to. We had spent an early honeymoon in a gloomy Scottish hotel and while George fished in the pouring rain I sat in the sombre lounge flipping through *Country Life* or *Trout and Salmon* and eating sour cauliflower cheese in the cold dining-room. At least, I thought, George was unlikely to be unfaithful while flogging the water.

Apart from fishing I tried to be everything to George and one way was by continually altering my appearance. I thought that if one day I was a blonde in blue satin and the next day a redhead in black leather with a feather boa, George could be fooled into thinking he had more than one woman.

CHAPTER 3

Trendy NW1

Dorothy was homesick for Wales, so we took a cottage there for the summer holidays. George could fish, Dorothy could meet her married lover, Jim's father, and I would take the children for picnics on the beach.

Outside the cottage was a stream where Patrick caught an eel, while Tom learnt to walk and Candy, aged three, who had just spent a month in hospital with a lung infection, played doctors and nurses. On the day that George caught four trout, she wrapped them in slices of bread, laid them out on the slate slab in the scullery and spooned cough medicine down their spiky little throats.

It must have been an unusually good summer because I loved Wales and I loved the cottage. By the time the holidays ended, I had persuaded George to take a Max Ernst off the wall and buy a place of our own.

'Gaer', as our cottage was called, was two miles from the sea and reached by a track that led from a farmhouse. The owners, a farmer and his wife, were very surprised by what we offered for the rather derelict building; but I had checked up on local prices and I offered £250 more than it was worth. I wanted it. The track was steep and rocky, but just possible for a car if you drove carefully. In the front of the cottage were fields and behind was a thicket that dropped down to a stream. There was an abandoned car that the children painted and made their own. Inside the cottage were two rooms downstairs and a kitchen. Upstairs were three small bedrooms. The loo was outside, but after George had told the children about an old tramp being found dead and frozen to the seat they wouldn't use it, so we built on a bathroom.

We also moved in London that year, 1964. Our Hampstead house was very small for three adults and four children, and one day, when we were at lunch with friends in Camden Town I noticed that the house next door to them was for sale. It had been an Irish lodging house and was in a very run-down state. But, once 'Mrs Perfect' had organised the sales, the architect and the builders, there would be a family room cum kitchen, a posh sitting-room with beige hessian on the walls and five bedrooms. I followed the NW1 style: William Morris birds flew round the bedrooms and forests spread up the stairs. Patrick's room had blue sky and clouds on the ceiling and green fields on the walls. We bought pine furniture from Fay Weldon's husband Ron, who had an antique shop in Primrose Hill. In Wales there was a large tumbling-down shack on the beach, where they sold furniture from house clearances, and there we found a brass bed with a five-foot high faded patterned headboard.

Every Saturday the residents of Gloucester Crescent, led

by George, and Jonathan Miller, would gather round Reg in the nearby street market. Reg also did house clearances and among the chipped saucepans and broken lights were treasures to be fought over. Competition was fierce for art nouveau objects and Victorian watercolours. 'Shillin,' Reg would shout, glancing quickly at an item being held up, or, more mysteriously, 'Ten shillin,' for a cracked pastry bowl.

'Who lives in Trendy NW1?' ran a headline in a daily paper. And the answer was Jonathan and Rachel Miller, Alan Bennett, Claire and Nick Tomalin, Professor A. J. Ayer and his wife Dee Wells, Alice Thomas Ellis and her publisher husband Colin Haycraft. We took turns with the school run. Dee Wells and I were the most popular drivers with the children, Dee because of her sense of humour and the ice creams she bought them all, and me because at nine o'clock

I was still in my nightie and let the girls brush my long tangly hair.

We read *Private Eye*, the *New Statesman,* the *Sunday Times* and the *Observer.* George was now writing his column about pop music for the *Observer.* The Small Faces, The Who and Them, whose lead singer was Van Morrison, all came and sat politely in our sitting-room while George took notes and I made coffee. It was the first time a posh paper had recognised popular culture and not everyone approved. The journalist Paul Johnson wrote a stinging attack on a Beatles concert, contrasting it with the advantages of learning Latin, and inexplicably complaining about the cheap lipstick worn by the fans. George replied, pointing out the inherent snobbery of Johnson's position. An acknowledged poly-math, George's opinions would be canvassed on art, jazz and all aspects of swinging London.

George and Mick had simultaneously decided to give up touring and the band. Mick wanted to spend more time with his young family. He now owned a grocery shop, while George found the broadcasting and writing he did often clashed with gigs. We should have had enough money, but his income was so precarious compared with what we spent that we often got rude letters from the bank; and once, casting around for something to sell that wasn't a picture, we even sold a silver tea service that had belonged to Maudie. George was also working hard on the book for Weidenfeld; my job was to track down everyone he mentioned and get them to sign a release form. Most people were fairly resigned about having their smelly armpits or sexual indiscretions described. Only one or two of the girls wanted their names changed. Liverpool Mary was one, she came down to London to see us and read her entry. I remember her sitting in the garden and saying to me, 'You've got three children, that's as many as I've had abortions.'

As well as helping George with the book – and as this was his first, he needed a great deal of encouragement – I catalogued all his records and made a tape of his favourites. He missed singing – nobody claps except the wife when you're writing – but we used to go to pubs in the East End where there was live entertainment and I would sidle up to the compère while George was in the loo and suggest he should be invited up to sing. Initially the compère would be reluctant, but after George's dramatic rendition of 'Frankie and Johnnie' in which he simulates oral sex and, in the finale, flings himself from the stage, he always got the applause that he deserved and badly needed. He was still just able to do a falsetto imitation of a woman's voice and for an encore he would stick beer bottles under his sweater to make it look as if he had breasts and sing a raucous number called 'Big Butter and Egg Man'.

Every Easter and summer holiday we drove to the cottage. In the days before the Severn Bridge this was a ten-hour drive and, with four children in the car, exhausting. Happily for me, it was also in the days before 'purple hearts' – as we called speed – were banned. I would arrive with my nerves singing and my eyes on stalks and the come-down was horrific.

With the help of a farmer I built a lean-to greenhouse on the side of the house. George could write his book there, but only after the sun had gone down, as otherwise he fried.

Granny Maudie came to stay – although I can't think where we put her – and made huge scenes when I forced the children into the freezing sea. She would stand trembling with rage on the water's edge proffering a towel and a ginger biscuit. There were local carnivals – Candy undressed as Lady Godiva on the farmer's pony, Patrick as St Francis with our dog Benny, and little Tom and Baby Jim (whom, quite unfairly, I'd come to hate) went as Tweedle Dum and Tweedle Dee. My dislike of Baby Jim was based on his always being car sick on the London to Wales journey and on the fact that all his clothes, including his nappies, were meticulously ironed by Dorothy. Tom's were not, which enraged Granny Maudie, and encouraged me to dress Tom like a gypsy. 'You'd think it was the other way round,' she'd say, 'Jim the little lord and Tom the servant's child.' 'Dorothy isn't a servant,' I would reply. But Maudie liked me and, in spite of her fussing over Tom, I liked her. She also loved Patrick and felt that we were not always kind to him. We weren't. After a day on the beach I discovered that Patrick had left his new Wellington boots behind. I was so horrible to him that without my knowing, he set off to walk the four miles there and back to find them, only to discover that the tide had come in and carried them out to sea.

On an old, and quite good, report of his from when he was nine, George has written, 'Patrick comes over as lazy but clever', and we didn't have a word of praise for his star for maths. When Patrick thought he'd discovered Adrian Henri's poems he was quickly put in his place and told that Adrian was one of George's oldest friends and that the four large black paintings hanging on the stairs were by him. Later on it was the same with Dylan or Hendrix. They were no good, only the early blues guitarists like Sonny Terry and Big Bill Broonzy knew how to play.

In London we went a lot to parties and once a fortnight we gave a dinner party. At one of these, Brian Epstein, the Beatles' manager, was so shocked by George's description of the semen-stained knickers which the police kept in their black museum that he got up and left. I didn't mind these stories: George was always very funny and it wasn't 'done' to be thought prudish.

I was photographed and interviewed for *Vogue*, giving my favourite recipes: pigeon pâté, osso bucco, crème brûlée for pudding (if the hot sugar curdled the mixture I would cry and start again). When he was tipsy, George would take off his clothes and act out his tableaux of Man, Woman and Bulldog. He would also sing obscene songs. Although this was popular with the majority of our guests, the one person who was shocked by Man, Woman and Bulldog was the American comedian Lenny Bruce. Lenny was the last person to be prosecuted for obscenity in the States. When he appeared at the Establishment Club George had written about him for Karl Miller, literary editor of the *New Statesman*: 'He is on the side of lovers and against the judge, the politician, the priest and the decent citizen for whom the sexual act is dirty, the whole disgusting crew who hang morons and test bombs. He is a black humourist in the authentic tradition. He swings like a Negro preacher. This small lemur-like creature spreads a formidable gospel.'

After this review, George had met Lenny back-stage. They got on well and one night we persuaded him to come back to our house along with some other friends. Soon it was cabaret time and George took off his clothes. He struck the pose of strong man (Charles Atlas), modest woman (hands over breasts) and then went down on all fours and, with his balls sticking out behind, backed towards the astonished Lenny. Perhaps Lenny would not have been so surprised if he had been less stoned and less drunk. But as it was, he thought we were all still at the Club and couldn't understand why, if people could stomach the sight of bare balls and a penis, they were so shocked by him? But the evening ended with an exchange of gifts. George gave Lenny a crucifix made out of a four-inch long brass bullet. Inexplicably, Lenny gave George a small alarm clock. The next time Lenny was invited to appear in London, he was turned back at the airport. Henry Brooke, the right-wing home secretary, was responsible, but Mary Whitehouse, the housewife guardian of the nation's morals, was also beginning to make her influence felt.

George was invited up to Manchester to engage in a censorship dialogue with Whitehouse and *Telegraph* journalist Peregrine Worsthorne. Worsthorne had been at school with George and, although a Conservative, didn't agree with Mrs Whitehouse or her husband and had been especially shocked by Mr Whitehouse declaring over and over again that 'hanging was the linchpin of British justice'.

Naturally I went with George, and I did all my Christmas shopping while they recorded the programme. The shopping, which consisted of presents for the children, confused Mr and Mrs Whitehouse, who seemed surprised that we were a family.

George had now joined the team on *The Critics*, a regular Sunday slot on the BBC Third Programme, now Radio 3. Four personalities were asked to read a book, see a film, a play and visit an art exhibition. They would then discuss each in turn. The contributors were intellectual heavyweights such as art critic David Sylvester, philosopher A. J. Ayer and critic Marganita Laski. Maudie was so overwhelmed with pleasure when she heard, that she put her hand on her heart and begged us to tell her that we weren't teasing. But when we told her that Lord Snowdon was coming to photograph us for a book on the London art scene, she took it very casually. He posed us in our tiny patio: in the photograph, Patrick is doing a complicated wooden puzzle on a marble-topped table with me looking on, Candy is naked and has her bum facing the camera, Tom is sitting in a plastic washing-up bowl and George is working on a small portable typewriter with a cigarette hanging out of his mouth. Off camera is a bottle of advocaat, a tipple that Snowdon had not come across before and was much surprised by. When the book was published we were invited to the launch party at Kensington Palace. Princess Margaret had belatedly remembered about wives: 'and your wife' was squeezed into the margin of her hand-written invitation. She came up to George to tell him how much she loved his strip cartoon, *Flook*, and then, turning to me, she said in her high-pitched clear voice, 'I hear we have something in common. We both started work at fourteen.'

George was also the *Observer*'s TV critic. I liked this. No longer could he be tempted into sinning with the Supremes or the likes of Sandy Shaw and Cilla Black. Television was wonderful in those days – *Z Cars*, *The Wednesday Play*, *That Was the Week That Was*, *Steptoe & Son* and *Till Death Us Do Part*. We had more money. As well as the TV column, there were two film scripts. One of them, *Smashing Time,* a comedy about Swinging London, starred David Hemmings, Rita Tushingham and Lynn Redgrave. It was a flop at the time but subsequently became something of a cult film.

Swinging London, Carnaby Street, miniskirts, feather boas and see-through tops caused me great anxiety. The only time I'd had breasts worth looking at was when I'd been feeding a baby. Mick Mulligan, George's band-leader, had once remarked, 'Not much happening on the tit scene.' Apparently I'd replied, 'Not your problem, Mick.' Jazz musicians, like a lot of men, are very keen on breasts. A flat-chested friend of mine told me that when she was going out with a trombonist, he had enjoyed humiliating her by running his hands all over her body and saying, 'This game is called Hunt the Tits.'

CHAPTER 4

Cracking Up

It never crossed my mind that I should get a job. Although many of my women friends with as many children did work, I was too busy painting on false eyelashes, sticking photographs in books and trailing George. We had engaged a secretary to type his book but I still managed to become indispensable to him. I had left school at fourteen, been a shop assistant, a cleaning lady and a night-club hostess as well as caring for my mother who was often very depressed. All these jobs had given me various skills, mostly of a traditionally feminine kind. Feminism, at least in Britain, was still in the wings.

At some moment in the mid-1960s my veneer started to crack and I became suicidal. I would lie in bed clasping razor blades and weeping for some forgotten reason until George came up to comfort me. Once a week I drove to the Haliwick hospital in north London and was given a lecture and anti-depressants by a strict Scottish psychiatrist. George would sit patiently in the waiting-room and then we would drive to Soho and have lunch at Wheeler's.

It wasn't my first experience of mental homes. In 1958, I came back from Afghanistan with hepatitis; Michael Alexander left me and I was admitted to hospital. The day after I was discharged, Anne Wollheim saw me wandering down the King's Road in Chelsea, probably looking rather thin. She took me back for tea and then, realising I had nowhere to live, offered me a home. Anne was married to the philosopher Richard Wollheim and had four children, two by her first marriage to Philip Toynbee. One Saturday when she was away visiting her daughter at boarding school, I took an overdose. I laid out fifteen pink sleeping pills in a neat row, and solemnly took them one by one. It was a gamble: it was enough to kill me but I also knew that Richard was in the house. He said that he was going out to dinner, but I must have thought it possible that he would come up to my room and say goodbye. He did, found me unconscious, called the ambulance and accompanied me to the hospital. They asked him for my age and other details, and when it came to the question 'What occupation?' Richard replied, 'None.' 'Oh really,' said the nurse, apparently looking very

surprised. 'What order is she from? We've never had a suicidal nun.' As professor of logic at London University, Richard loved this exchange.

From the hospital in central London I had been taken to Banstead, a mental home in the suburbs. As the ambulance drove away I looked out through the bars on the window and watched Anne Wollheim and Michael Alexander waving goodbye to me. Anne was standing with her back to Michael, making it very obvious that she held him responsible and wouldn't speak to him.

I was put into a bright, clean dormitory with four beds on each side of the room. The next morning I had a short interview with a doctor who asked me to sign a form agreeing to treatment. I was then given an aspirin, told to lie on a bed and bite on a bit of rubber. A contraption resembling headphones was then placed on my head and I was given electric shock treatment. Although ECT, as it was called, knocked you unconscious, it was in the days before patients were first given an anaesthetic, and not only was the treatment painful, but you came round with a splitting headache and no short-term memory.

This time the Scottish doctor at the Haliwick, although she prescribed me many different drugs, made no suggestion of shock treatment and at least I had a partner who was kind and loving – if somewhat bewildered by my irrational moods.

On one occasion we were at a party of the Tynans' when I became overwhelmed with desperation and panic. Ken Tynan was famous not only for his brilliant theatre reviews, but also because he was the first person to say 'fuck' on

British TV. We had been watching the programme with Jonathan Miller and his wife, Rachel, when Tynan let the word drop casually into the conversation. George rang the BBC to congratulate them.

The party was very glamorous – Mike Nichols and Marlene Dietrich were there. Dietrich had been complaining about the vulgarity of the miniskirt when suddenly and for no obvious reason I thought if I stayed I might explode. The ground seemed to be tipping away from me like something in a painting before perspective was discovered. No one noticed me leaving, and I drove to London Airport and checked into a motel. I sat frozen on the bed, but slowly the explosive feelings began to subside. It was as if I had been under water with my lungs bursting and my heart and blood racing, but now everything was slowing down and returning to a more normal state. I rang George. He came in a minicab, thinking I would not want to drive home alone, and brought a warm coat and some Valium. I felt very foolish, and as usual after one of those attacks I couldn't understand why it had happened.

It was the same when seemingly small things went wrong. Once, when travelling back by train from Wales, I had left our picnic lunch of chicken and Chablis on the kitchen table. When I discovered its loss, I sat hunched and despairing, slumped in the corner seat while George leapt out at every station scouring the platform for an open buffet. It was Sunday, it was Wales, and it was the 1960s: we went hungry.

I had also developed an obsession about my knickers. I had Welsh ones and London ones and I bought paper ones to wear between the two places. The night before our departure, the cottage was cleaned and tidied and everyone's clothes laid out in piles. But the paper knickers had fallen on the floor and it was George's job to gather the rubbish and incinerate it. He took down the waste-paper basket from the bedroom and the knickers went up in smoke. I realised what had happened and refused to get out of bed. George knew better than to try to reason with me, and had he been able to drive I'm sure he would have searched the pharmacies of west Wales to buy some.

George's patience with me was heroic. He loved me very much but I could never feel certain that he did, or that I was safe with him. I once pretended to run away and hid under the bed so that I could watch him looking for me. He rang some close friends, called my name in the garden and then sat down, just a few feet away from me, sighed, and poured himself a large whisky. I crawled out, rather dusty, and George got me the bottle of Valium, mother's little helper.

Sometimes the television could spark a reaction in me that was out of proportion. *In Two Minds*, a Laingian play by David Mercer about a girl made schizophrenic by her uncaring family, and *Talking to a Stranger* by John Hopkins, also about a dysfunctional family, I found very disturbing. *Talking to a Stranger* was in four parts, each episode told from the point of view of the four family members, and each one ending with a different interpretation for the mother's suicide. I thought I might be going that way, and in a sane moment decided to get some proper help.

Miss Thomas was a Freudian analyst. She lived in a large maisonette near Primrose Hill and I saw her three times a week. After she had let me in with an intercom, I would wait for her in a room that was underneath her bathroom, and I could quite plainly hear her peeing and the loo flushing. Then, leaning over the banisters, she would say 'You can come up now, Diana'. I always imagined that she was smiling down at me. Often I felt so faint when I was there that like the Cheshire cat, her face and body seemed to disappear and only her smile was visible to me. She once asked me if the sound of her urinating embarrassed me. It did, but I denied it.

Miss Thomas was tall, aged about sixty and looked like the sort of teacher that girls not only adore but are slightly in awe of. Sometimes, when my fifty minutes was up, standing by the door she would say something off the record, like 'Don't worry, you'll be all right.' But I can't remember much else. I do remember clinging on to the rather hard chaise longue that I lay on; at times it would buck and sway under me and then I would ask if I could get up. Miss Thomas would then move from her chair, which of course was behind my head and sit behind her desk with me opposite her. She had kind, pale blue eyes. Some things I could only tell her if I could see her face – like Jonathan Miller's imitation of her. He had never met her, but knowing that Miss Thomas was Australian was enough, and in a Barry Humphries voice he would launch into psychobabble over the dinner table.

Then I lost the use of my legs. It had been an ordinary evening, children tucked up in bed, Patrick doing his homework, dinner cleared away, and I sat down to watch the news. An African in Rhodesia who had offended his government had been hanged. Many people had marched and campaigned on his behalf to no avail. I too had marched, but

I thought I had to identify more closely or I had no right to care. It occurred to me that if I took an overdose and was stomach-pumped, the action of swallowing the tube would be similar to strangulation. Upstairs I swallowed all my Valium and called for George to come up. I explained carefully to him, and to the ambulance men and the nurses and doctors, that it wasn't a suicide, but an attempt to identify with the hanged African. I also apologised for causing so much trouble. They put me in a ward and kept me there for a couple of days. The doctors told George that they had not found any traces of Valium or any other similar substance in my stomach. Miss Thomas, George and the doctor considered getting me sectioned, but Miss Thomas said she would try and cope for a bit longer. When it was time for me to leave hospital it was discovered that I couldn't walk. George carried me, and for the next month carried me three times a week to Miss Thomas.

During that month I thought that if I could visit the convent where I had been a boarder during the war I might remember things that would help me and cure my paralysis. The nuns seemed unsurprised by George and his burden. Every now and then he sat me down on a window ledge to get his breath back. One nun said she remembered me, but as thirty years had passed I think she was just being kind. When my brother Alan came to see me he said, 'Of course she remembered you, you were always running away.'

I stayed in bed for six weeks, and then, one day when George had brought me up some lunch, he hovered at the door and asked if there was anything I wanted. 'Yes,' I said, 'go down and sack Dorothy.'

This was a horrible request. Dorothy had been with us for nearly five years: Tom and Jim, who were almost the same age, were like brothers; Dorothy had her own flat at the top of the house and ran a nursery school in the family room; her lover came to stay and also her friends. For some reason I had come to hate her.

Turning Dorothy out of her home was harsh, but she too had become very neurotic and when George gave her notice he explained that he could only deal with one mad woman, and it had to be me.

Dorothy was given six months' notice. Luckily her skills at managing babies and small children were known and admired in NW1. Also, as many of the mothers worked, her skills were needed and Dorothy soon found rooms where she could run a crèche. Unluckily for me it was opposite our house, and when she finally left, although I no longer had to eat dinner with her I had to organise my shopping so that we didn't meet at the butcher's.

Poem of Love and Hope

For Diana

The grown-up girl I love,
Whose stomach bears the stretch-marks of three children,
Whose least gesture can surprise me into tenderness,
Whose arms have encircled me for six years,
Whose physical presence evokes a wall in Wales or certain
    rooms in London,
The grown-up girl I love is pegged down like a Gulliver,
The prisoner of a thousand tiny shadows.

I cannot hope to fight with these small gentry.
They move as fast as flies, and if I grab one
Another six come buzzing to replace it
From the world's dung-heap. Such a course is futile.

Besides, I know they are emissaries
Whose master's in another world more secret
Than their loud day-to-day. A suburban landscape,
Whose birds are long since dead, whose leaves have fallen.
Their master is a small deserted girl,
Whose pain, and fear, and sense of desolation
Have made her want to try to kill my wife.

She isn't stupid. Pain has made her cunning.
She's mastered every clever shabby skill.
She's a ventriloquist, a puppet master,
A con-man, practised liar and dissembler,

Can pass forged cheques or issues worthless bonds,
And yet she cannot win, and for one reason:
I know she's there and she knows that I know it.

I arm myself, am on perpetual watch.
My eyes are trained to spot her stealthy movements,
Behind my wife's eyes, dazed as a wax doll.
I have my allies too,
Warm friends, and a tall expert at the head of stairs,
Whose plants are used to victories slow as theirs.

But above all what will defeat this phantom
Is love, not for my wife who is her victim,
But for herself, the small unhappy creature,
And in the light, what she believes are evil,
Never-to-be-forgotten, death if spoken,
Will seem just what they are: poor baby monsters,
Laid by stupidity, hatched by adult circumstance,
With teeth so small they cannot break the skin.
And from that moment
The child can grow and so become the woman
She thinks she wants to hurt, and I can love
Not one nor yet the other, but them both;
Kiss the tired, happy child and then turn to my wife.

George Melly, 1966

CHAPTER 5

There Was an Old Woman

There was an old woman who lived in a shoe,
She had so many children she didn't know what to do.

In 1967, during the six months when Dorothy was working out her notice, two more children came to live with us – Joshua and Caroline Bowler. George and I had been staying with the writer Emma Tennant at her cottage in Wiltshire when she got a phone call from the writer Francis Wyndham.

He told her that Henrietta Moraes, Joshua and Caroline's mother, had been arrested for attempted burglary: she had begun using heroin and needed money. The burglary was not well planned. Henrietta had tried to climb up an ancient drainpipe which was only flimsily attached to a house in Hampstead. She fell noisily to the ground, the police were called and the following morning she was remanded in custody. The children, aged ten and eleven, were left 'home alone'.

When Henrietta was married to Dom Moraes the poet, she and I had become close friends. She was formidable: dark, attractive, clever, cruel, witty and often quite overpowering. Numerous artists including Francis Bacon and Lucien Freud had painted her.

In 1960, after the Sharpeville massacre, Henrietta and I had taken a taxi to South Africa House. A crowd of noisy students were demonstrating outside, but the police held them back to let us through; we were so elegantly dressed that the police thought we just wanted to reach the pavement. We took milk bottles from our handbags and threw them through the plate-glass windows. The glass shattered, the startled police moved forward and we were bundled into a waiting van.

At the station they stripped us of everything personal and anything that we could injure ourselves with. It was a long night and our hangovers were beginning, but we sang to each other in our adjoining cells and the next morning Frank Norman, the ex-criminal and writer of *Fings Ain't What They Used To Be* came and paid Henrietta's fine. He didn't pay mine, but then he loved Henrietta – so did I.

Recently I had seen less of her. Rumours of hard drugs and shop-lifting had circulated and I had begun to feel intimidated by her. George and I drove back to London and over to Henrietta's flat in Battersea to gather up the children. When we got home camp beds and sleeping bags were found and spaces made in Tom and Candy's rooms.

While Henrietta was in Holloway Prison, her probation officer, Miss Patterson, came to see the children. She told us that they would not be allowed to go home until the court was satisfied that certain conditions were met. The gas and electricity bills must be paid so that the services could be reconnected and, more important, the young heroin addicts who were living in Henrietta's flat must be found alternative accommodation.

We drove over to Battersea with our good intentions and found a young couple in bed making love. This seemed rather surprising as we had always heard that heroin addicts lost all of their appetites. We left them in bed and cleaned the flat, which was cold and squalid. Dirty plates and cups overflowed from the sink on to the floor, congealed messes had hardened and grown interestingly in the saucepans. The lack of hot water didn't make the cleaning any easier – nor did a broken vacuum cleaner. But the most important task was disposing of the hypodermics and other evidence of drugs.

Finally, four hours later and with the flat in a reasonable state, we bundled the couple into the car and, once home, installed them in Tom's room while we rang round to find them somewhere to live. Eventually a bed-sit in Muswell Hill was found and I went upstairs to tell them. They were slightly worried that it wasn't on the Piccadilly Line, as they had to go to Boots in Piccadilly Circus for their heroin. Collecting the drugs presented a problem for them. The law allowed addicts to collect their prescription every twenty-four hours; the girl – and she couldn't have been more than seventeen – could collect after midday and the boy after midnight: two trips and lots of fares. They couldn't bear to be separated from each other, nor could either of them get through the twelve hours of withdrawal to synchronise their habit.

It was amazing what they had done to Tom's room in the time it had taken me to find the bed-sit. The bed had been stripped and they were sitting on the floor wrapped in blankets and playing with Lego. A sheet had been hung across the window to blot out the evening sun – presumably they had been unable to operate the Venetian blind. The air was thick with cigarette smoke and they looked very happy.

George found them an old leather suitcase of his father's, and we transferred their meagre belongings into it from their carrier bags. In the back of the car George sat and silently scratched away the luggage label which had our address on it.

Their new landlady was middle-aged, neat and respectable, her suburban house was spotless, with bright floral wallpaper and a mantelpiece crowded with china cats. On a shiny sideboard were some framed photographs of a young couple with a baby. 'My son,' she said when she saw me looking at it, 'with his little boy. I haven't seen him yet, they've gone to Australia.'

We explained that her new tenants had been ill and needed to rest a lot. She seemed quite un-worried by their appearance, smiled at them, said she could see they needed feeding up, and offered to get them some tea. I wished them good luck, and not knowing of George's desire for anonymity, wrote out our address for them. I rang up a month later; they were still there and fine.

The next task was to get the bills paid and the services reconnected. Henrietta was still in prison on remand, but, assuming she wouldn't get a sentence for the failed break-in of the Hampstead house, she would soon be out.

With fairly hefty bills, phone, gas and so on, we needed

£1,000 to settle everything. I made a list of her friends who might help. It wasn't difficult; I wasn't the only one who loved Henrietta: in one way or another Francis Bacon, Sonia Orwell, David Sylvester did too. Some admired her spirit in attempting to climb the rotten drainpipe during the attempted burglary. Everyone was generous, the bills were paid, and there was £100 over for Henrietta. We went over to the flat for a final clean, I found one more hypodermic under a cushion and proudly showed Miss Patterson round.

But the children didn't go back. Henrietta came out and disappeared. When Miss Patterson caught up with her she was busy spending the £100 on heroin and furious with us for having spent *her* money, given to *her* by *her* friends on stupid things like gas and electricity. Then she came to stay with us. She would follow me round the house with what had started life as a cup of coffee in her hand; it was given little treats – a drop of vodka in the sitting-room, a splash of wine in the kitchen and sometimes a little lager. In the sitting-room, where she had a mattress on the floor, she would sit cross-legged playing *Sergeant Pepper* over and over again, while I was bidden to find her false eyelashes which hid like spiders in the carpet.

The summer holidays came and as Henrietta had disappeared again we decided to take all the children to Wales but leave Jim and Dorothy, who still had two months of her notice to complete, behind. I realised that this time it would be a problem to get George to the river to fish; he fished for sea trout on a stretch of the Teifi that was seven or eight miles away from the cottage. In previous years, with Dorothy looking after the children, I had avoided her

company by driving George to the river and waiting for him
until he wanted to come home. If the evenings were light
enough I sat in the car and read, otherwise I listened to the
radio: Jimmy Young, Tony Hancock and Frankie Howerd.
Howerd had once appeared at the Establishment Club when
George was on first. George told a few jokes between his
songs, but Howerd made a fuss and told George to stick to
the blues – *he* was to be the only comedian.

With Dorothy left behind in London, I couldn't think
how I was to get George to the river without leaving the
children alone. The answer came in the shape of a Solex, a
small French moped more like a bicycle than a motor bike,
which I'd seen a photograph of in *Vogue*. George was thrilled
with his machine. It took him four attempts over two years
to pass his test – on one occasion he failed to notice his
instructor stepping out from between two cars and ran over
his foot.

It wasn't difficult having so many children to look after – at least they were never bored. Candy and Caroline were one team and the older boys took care of Tom, who was six.

The holiday was a huge success. I was too busy to hide under the bed, to run away leaving no one to take care of the children was unthinkable. They all learned to ride and they fished in the little stream. At the village carnival Candy and Caroline went as mermaids, Joshua and Patrick as Rolling Stones – hand-cuffs and dirty T-shirts – and Tom went as a Roman warrior. Henrietta came to stay for a few days and astonished the farmer's wife by blowing into horses' nostrils, explaining that that was how you communicated with animals. Catastrophe was averted when one of the children smelt smoke before Henrietta's abandoned cigarette nearly burned the house down. A large Edwardian wooden cot, that Tom and Candy still loved to sleep in, bore the scars.

Miss Patterson had become a good friend. She and I wondered what would happen to the children in September. Boarding school was mentioned and Sonia Orwell suggested approaching Caroline's godmother, the writer Caroline Blackwood, for help. Little Caroline had been named after her godmother, who was rich and had been a good friend of Henrietta's. Caroline was then married to the composer Israel Citkovitz, having been divorced from Lucian Freud, but not yet married to Robert Lowell. She was willing to pay for Caroline to go to Frensham Heights, a progressive boarding school, but on two conditions: Henrietta must never be told that she was footing the bill and I was to get little Caroline assessed by an educational psychologist to confirm that boarding school was right for her. Uneasily I found one and took Caroline along for the interview. Understandably Henrietta was furious and I couldn't tell her that it wasn't my idea. Nevertheless Caroline went to Frensham and so did her brother. Joshua didn't have a rich godfather, but we appealed to the head of Frensham and, backed up by letters from Richard Hoggart and Jonathan

Miller, Joshua too was accepted, and without fees.

Caroline had formed a close relationship with me and I knew I would miss her. Joshua was more of a problem: he had made friends with a thirty-year-old American whom he and Henrietta had met in Hyde Park. The American, Ted, had offered to help with Josh, take him to football matches and the cinema. Once, when we went to pick Josh up at Ted's flat, George remarked on the prints and drawings of half-naked young men, but none of them were of boys as young as Josh and so we just assumed that Ted was homosexual. Although George made jokes about Ted liking Josh, neither of us realised till much later that he was raping him. With hindsight it should have been fairly obvious, but in those days though we made jokes about scoutmasters, we hadn't heard of paedophile rings, and we had no inkling of what Josh was going through.

At the end of August, before their departure for Frensham Heights, Caroline and Josh went back to their Battersea flat and Miss Patterson came to tell me that Henrietta no longer trusted me and that I was not to try to see the children. Luckily for me Miss Thomas's summer holiday was also over, my sessions were resumed and she helped me to deal with the loss of the children, and of Henrietta. No matter how much George tried to reassure me, I felt guilty and thought that Henrietta had been right in suspecting me of trying to keep her children – or at least trying to steal their love.

CHAPTER 6

Miss Thomas's Prediction

During the two years after Joshua and Caroline left, Patrick became a troubled teenager. When he was twelve he was interviewed by journalist Maureen Cleave in the *Evening Standard* for a series of articles about young people. He told her that he would like to be a famous research chemist and find a cure for cancer and another for drug addiction. Cleave described him as being tall and thin, remarkably handsome with graceful movements and fine blue eyes. She went on to say that he taught George to play chess, loved babies, cooked omelettes, liked the Egyptian room at the British Museum, read Sherlock Holmes and although he didn't believe in God, sang in a church choir. She said he had a demanding and argumentative intelligence and viewed his inevitable marriage with comic and elaborate resignation.

But in 1970, aged fifteen, like many teenagers he was experimenting with cannabis and other forms of rebellion. One afternoon we were rung by the police, who said that he

had been arrested on an Irish demonstration with a bomb. Fortunately they believed his story that he was carrying it for a person he'd never met before; but he should have been at school and the headmaster confirmed that he often missed lessons.

As parents we were very strict in our way; we didn't negotiate or suggest ways in which Patrick could earn more freedom, so he pushed harder and was always being punished. Carefully rolled joints were found in his room, so going to a pop festival that weekend was out of bounds. Empty milk bottles put back in the fridge meant extra washing up. His friends moved through the house, not as individuals but as one body, leaving the house like a deserted battlefield. When they'd gone I never knew whether to be relieved that the moans of Bessie Smith had succeeded the rage of The Who, or to be fearful of where they'd gone and what they might be doing. George still wrote for *Peace News*,

but our house was a war zone; he still said that he was
an anarchist, but together we formed a very authoritarian
alliance.

Dorothy and Baby Jim had finally left and we had a very
nice Swiss au pair living with us. She was only responsible for
babysitting for Tom and Candy and in 1971, when Patrick's
headmaster asked us to take Patrick away from his comprehensive, we decided he must go to boarding school once his
O levels were done.

We choose Monkton Wylde, a progressive co-
educational school on the south coast with no head master
or mistress. Attending lessons was voluntary. The school
didn't employ domestic staff or cooks and the children,
along with the teachers, had to manage their own meals and
the cleaning. Many of the children who went there came
from schools which found it impossible to deal with them;
some were paid for by local authorities. It was a brave
attempt by the school to find an alternative way of teaching
'problem' children. Eventually Patrick loved it. His reports –
rather surprisingly they did have them – said things like, 'He
is working well and we hope he is enjoying things as much as
he seems to be.'

Patrick was due to start boarding in September and that
summer we were invited to the South of France to stay with
some American friends. I persuaded George that a holiday
all together out of the Welsh rain would be good. Reluctantly
George agreed, and we went shopping for some suitable
clothes for him. He has always been a dandy, but it was one
of our over-drawn months and at first we didn't know where
to find anything cheap enough. Then one day, after a typical

Soho lunch at Wheeler's (we were never too broke for that), we stopped by a shop on Old Compton Street catering for the restaurant trade, and there in the window were some smart waiter's outfits: blue and white striped trousers and crisp white cotton jackets. George loved the look and bought three sets.

The house was near St Tropez. It had a large swimming pool and a cottage. Our American friends, Jane and Joan, who had rented the villa, slept in the main house. George and I, plus Tom and Candy slept in the annexe, while Patrick and the teenage daughters of Jane and Joan slept in the cottage.

It was too hot for George, but for the rest of us the sea was near, and if we couldn't be bothered to drive there we lay around the pool. The only problem was our lack of money. George had written the scripts for two films. Neither had been successful, but before we realised that Hollywood wasn't going to beckon we had wildly over-spent. Jane and Joan had lots of money and the dinners in St Tropez and the lunches on the beach were ruinous; we were relieved when our friends got bored with St Tropez and left for two weeks in Italy. George was bored too. Every day his afternoon sleep went on for longer while I took the children to the beach.

Miss Thomas had always said that with analysis my dependency on George would diminish and my marriage would change. One afternoon her prediction began to be fulfilled.

George not only loved me, but he had cared for me and looked after me in a way that my mother had not been able to. Like a child rejecting and rebelling against its parents, I was now about to do just that to him.

I came back from the beach to find George sitting on the terrace with two young men. One was fair and looked like a young Mick Jagger and the other was dark and looked like Pete Townsend. They had arrived on bikes and were looking for Cathy, Jane's teenage daughter. George said the boys were hungry and would I find them something to eat. I brought out bread and cheese (no butter, too expensive) and some Coca-Cola and was then furious when George said they could stay for supper and spend the night.

That evening we sat around on the terrace while Max, the

blond one, played Beatles songs on Cathy's guitar and I fell in love with him. Not until ten years later did I learn that George had too.

Max was eighteen and had dropped out of school – he wasn't sure what he wanted to do. Steve, the dark one, knew that he would be a sculptor. The following morning I had to take our car into town for repair. Max came with me and we walked back along the beach holding hands.

George invited Max and Steve to stay on until Jane and Joan returned and he encouraged me to flirt with Max. He only meant to send me out to play for a little while before returning safely home. He also hoped to watch our games, perhaps to join in some of them, but rebellion doesn't necessarily follow the wishes of the elders and George was devastated when I swiftly excluded him.

I had never been in love with anyone young before: all three husbands had been ten years older than me, and some lovers much more than that. Max became as infatuated with me as I was with him, and although we did nothing more than hold hands and gaze at each other, it was obvious to everyone that something was up.

We were leaving in two days to return to Wales where we were to spend the rest of the summer holidays. Embarrassingly I had taken to not wearing shoes, and on the station platform where we went to load the car on to the train for Calais, I cut my foot badly on a piece of glass. This gave me the excuse to sit and cry, but George knew that it was leaving Max which provoked the flood.

The cottage in Wales seemed cold and charmless, but the children were pleased to be back. They were excited by the prospect of the local river carnival that was to take place the next day – Tom particularly, as I had said he could take part in the swimming race. He had only just learnt to swim in France and George was reluctant to allow it, but misery and frustration made me careless and I overrode his objections.

It was raining again the next day and the river was dark brown and flowing fast. All the children stood shivering on a boat anchored in the middle of the river, and a man shouted 'Jump!' Ten little children jumped, but only nine little heads came up. Everyone on the bank stood up and someone shouted, 'The little blonde girl hasn't come up.' I knew they meant Tom, who had long wispy blond hair. And then there he was, bobbing about in the water. He said afterwards that he had gone under the boat and had held his breath until he could feel his way out. In the pub that night everyone was talking about it and some were asking, 'How could his mother have let him – a little thing like that?' How indeed.

We were both relieved that, in two days' time, we would be back in London.

George fished and went to the pub, getting drunk quite often. The weather stayed cold and I sat on the beach, wrapped in a raincoat, watching the children refusing to swim in the cold sea. I sulked and longed for Max and the sun.

Max returned at the end of September, but there were two reasons why we couldn't have sex: he had the clap, and he felt he needed George's permission. The clap was cured, George gave his permission and we started an affair. I followed Max around, watching him play football, and spent the evenings smoking dope with his friends. George sat at home with the television. He was still the *Observer*'s TV critic and he was lonely.

On occasions he was still asked to sing with a band, and one night, with Max driving and me in the front passenger seat, we arrived in Weybridge at the gig. In the interval I left George and Max talking and went to the Ladies. There was a long queue and when I got back, George was drunk and Max was nowhere to be seen. He had told Max that he too was in love with him, but at the time I didn't know what had been said. George did his second set and we drove back to London in silence.

CHAPTER 7

Release

That September Patrick started his first term at
Monkton Wylde and I drove him down to the school.
On the lonely drive back I felt relief that he was safe and no
longer a source of worry to me. But with Tom and Candy at
school all day, and no longer compelled to glue myself to
George, I had very little to do and I was restless.

The affair with Max had given me a taste of what my
teens could have been like, and my on-going rejection of
George became part of trying to grow up. There were better,
kinder ways of doing that, but I didn't look for them or find
them.

That winter I began working for Release.

Release was an organisation started in 1967 by Rufus
Harris and Caroline Coon as a direct response to the number
of young people who were being arrested for possession of
drugs. Caroline and Rufus, with the help of sympathetic
solicitors, made sure that those charged were made aware of
their rights and, when possible, were legally represented. The

organisation was soon dealing with other problems: unwanted pregnancies, homelessness, immigration and adverse reaction to drugs; it had become an alternative legal and welfare centre.

By 1971 there was a staff of six, mostly attractive women in their late teens or early twenties. They wore long velvet dresses and worked for a pittance. Notting Hill, where the offices were situated, would later become a posh part of London, but then it was fairly grim. The stairs were filthy, the dustbins overflowed, the sink was always full of cups, and the old-fashioned gas fires had lost the parts that would have enabled them to give out a little heat. It was obvious what Mrs Perfect's tasks would be. So while Edith, my Swiss au pair, cooked the evening meal for Tom and Candy and ran the house, I swept the stairs, emptied ashtrays and bought dustbin bags and Nescafé for Release.

There were four rooms, one where people waited to be seen (we didn't call them clients or patients), one a private room for the doctors to use, one an office-cum-kitchen, and there was a big room where Caroline and Rufus worked.

Also in Princedale Road were the offices of *Oz*, an underground magazine started by Richard Neville, Felix Dennis and Jim Anderson. It was rude, subversive and anti-authoritarian. Until 1970 it stayed out of trouble, but in April of that year it advertised for some young people to produce their own issue. The authorities leapt on number 28, 'The School Kids' Issue': there was a cartoon showing Rupert Bear with a hard-on, a photograph of a young girl under the heading 'Jail Bait of the Month' and a picture of a schoolmaster masturbating. The case came to trial the following year. John Mortimer represented the defence, and George, along with other like-minded people, was a witness for the defence. The three defendants, having first been found guilty and sent to jail, were freed on appeal.

That autumn when I started work, Caroline and Rufus were engaged in helping the defence by organising a benefit to raise money. They had been given the first night of the film *Performance*, and we had to sell a lot of tickets. It wasn't easy – most of the Release friends only had enough money for a 'ha'porth' of dope on a Saturday night. Also some of the more difficult 'clients' felt they were entitled to a freebie. Jack, the archetypal tramp who smelt very bad and gave us all nits, was desperate to attend such a glamorous affair with Mick Jagger and all the other stars. Needles, one of our more unstable junkies, held Rufus at knife-point until he was convinced that there were no tickets in the building. Needles was tall and had a manic gleam, but although Rufus was slight and tiny he managed that situation easily and calmly.

I helped quite a lot with the ticket sales and soon after the premiere I began to fund-raise in other ways. For some time Release had been trying to get charitable status which would make it possible to apply to certain organisations for grants. I recruited various friends to form a committee: Sonia, the widow of George Orwell, Michael White the impresario, Richard Wollheim the philosopher, Peter Mond (later Lord Melchett of Greenpeace) and Michael Schofield the sociologist.

The main source of funds up until 1971 had been donations from schools and colleges, and subscriptions to the monthly newsletter. Sometimes the charismatic Caroline

Coon persuaded pop groups, such as Led Zeppelin, to do a Release benefit.

There were unexpected gifts too: Roman Polanski had given his friend Victor Lownes a gold cast of a cock, but they had fallen out and we had been given the heavy, shiny item to sell. None of us had the slightest idea how to dispose of it, and how to make money out of the golden penis was a topic discussed at every fund-raising meeting for years. I've often wondered what happened to it.

Once we had gained our charitable status we were able to raise the funds for a salary for a resident psychiatric social worker. Our first one was known as 'Spooks'. His main qualification for the job was having been a patient of Release, but as well as having a lot of sympathy for our troubled clients, he was also very depressed. One day he didn't come in and later that week he was discovered in bed full of barbiturates, with a plastic bag over his head. He left a letter requesting that Van Morrison be played at his funeral and that he should be buried in a kaftan. Emma Tennant had once given George a glamorous turquoise and gold one, and as he hadn't worn it for some time, I took it from his cupboard and Spooks, beautifully attired, was laid to rest with Van Morrison singing 'Astral Weeks'. After that experience, more conventionally qualified social workers were employed.

Apart from helping women to get abortions, either through the NHS or our friendly private abortionists, and arranging solicitors to deal with all the drug busts, an essential part of Release's work was the newsletter and manning the emergency phone line.

The newsletter was mainly written by Rufus, Caroline and Don Aitkin. Don was a brilliant chemistry student from Oxford. He seldom came into the office; I don't think the atmosphere suited him, but he knew more about the law than most lawyers and more about drugs than the Home Office.

The emergency phone line was organised by Penny who was head girl to Caroline's head mistress. A list of volunteers was drawn up every week and at the end of each day the office phones would be switched over to a volunteer's home. In the morning one had to remember to switch it back. We all had an emergency phone file which, as well as listing the phone numbers of our solicitors and doctors, also gave practical advice so that if the one call that an arrested person was allowed was to us, we would be able to deal with it correctly. Naturally the solicitors, who often nobly took the phone, were best at that, but if it was someone having a bad LSD trip they probably weren't so skilled.

One night, when it was my turn, the phone rang at about two a.m. and a young man said he thought he had just killed his girlfriend. He said he had left her lying on the floor of their flat and that he was now in a phone box in Ladbroke Grove. He refused to give me his address, but I told him to call an ambulance and go back to wait for them. I lay there wondering what to do, but half an hour later he rang again and said that she was certainly dead and therefore there was no point in calling an ambulance. This time, he did give me his address, so I rang the ambulance myself. Some time later that night the police rang me and said that an elderly couple lived at the address given and there was no sign of a body.

The next morning I drove up Ladbroke Grove and stopped at the house. Opposite was a phone box and I went and stood in it, trying to imagine the state of mind that would make someone imagine they had killed their girlfriend. It *was* imagined, because the police told me that no unexplained body was ever found in that area.

I stopped sharing a bed with George, and the emergency phone was partly responsible: he snored rhythmically but very loudly and on the nights when I had to listen for the phone I couldn't wear my ear plugs. I began to sleep in the sitting-room, and until we moved and had separate bedrooms, that was where I stayed.

In addition to charitable status, Release got a Home Office grant for non-charitable expenditure. We could now afford headed paper, T-shirts, badges and posters, all printed with our logo – a dove of peace. Fund-raising became easier, because as well as having things to sell, we looked more professional. Not all the staff liked this or my bossiness and I was not universally popular. One morning a staff meeting was called with one of our psychiatrists, Justin Schlicht, presiding, while Paul, my enemy No. 1, read out a six-page diatribe of my faults. These were mostly complaints about my age (at thirty-four I was at least ten years older than anyone else), my lack of street credibility, my spending too much on publicity and my unreasonable insistence on the staff turning up on time. Little Nell, who had recently come to work at Release, told me later that no one would have realised how shaken I felt, because I listened to people taking sides, while sitting on the biggest desk, swinging my legs and painting rainbows on my eyelids.

I had offered Little Nell the job after meeting her at our house one night, when her boyfriend, the painter Martin Sharp, brought her to dinner. When we had finished eating, she got up on the table and tap-danced among the coffee cups. It was spectacular and I employed her to be in charge of what was known as our 'hospitality room'. I felt that this gloomy place, where our clients waited among the dirty cups and ashtrays, would be pleasanter and more welcoming with Nell's sparkling personality. It wasn't a total success. Nell, who was Australian, got easily depressed by the seeming inability of our clients to improve their lot and she soon left to become famous as Columbia in *The Rocky Horror Show*.

Luckily I did have one lucrative project which secured my position. Richard Hamilton, Jim Dine and David Hockney all agreed to make a print each, which they gave us to sell. We made a lot of money immediately. As with other fund-raising ideas, George's name and reputation had been a great help and he loved being included and needed. He was also much happier now that he was the film critic for the *Observer* and no longer had to sit alone in front of the TV. Films for the press were shown in the morning. He went out more and started to have affairs. He told me that he had always been longing to, but had been too nervous of the effect it would have on me. He confessed that he was so bored with being faithful that he had promoted my affair with Max and was only upset to find himself excluded.

I was also having another affair. Most of the women at Release, including me, worshipped the doctors, and as there were never enough chairs for everyone, we were always, quite literally, sitting at their feet. I sat at the feet of a GP called Mel Henry, told him about my friend Ginger who had become addicted to heroin, and quite soon Mel and I were an item. He was only 5 foot 6, my height, Jewish and difficult. He played the jazz trombone, admired George, and had the most enormous chip on both shoulders. Three times a week I went to his flat in Barnes, cooked a meal, listened to yet more jazz, and drove home at six a.m. to be there before the children woke.

There were now three lots of shopping to manage: fish fingers and ice cream in one bag; tea bags, milk, sugar and paper clips in Release's; Mel ate only lean mince and kidney beans. A fantasy was kept up that when the children were older I would leave George and become 'a doctor's wife'. When Mel moved to a larger flat we went shopping together for furniture, bed linen and china and so forth. His taste was far more modern than mine – no rough pine, darned linen sheets or cracked Victorian plates. But I liked that, I liked pretending to be a quite different person. Miss Thomas, whom I stopped seeing after Max, had said that I was like a cipher that anyone could fill with whatever they liked.

Release was always invited to pop festivals, and although these were hard work everyone wanted to go, we drew lots for the person who had to stay in London and man the office and the emergency phone. I had a camper van with bunk beds so Tom and Candy usually came with me (although Candy hated the smelly toilets). Once there, we would set up our tents: the legal tent where the solicitors sat, and the bad-trip tent. Usually only people with personal experience of acid worked in the trip tent, which was hung with soft velvet drapes and had a mattress and cushions spread out on the rather damp floor. Little cans of bubble blow and incense were kept on a decorated orange box and Ravi Shankar's music played quietly. Many young people took LSD at festivals and it wasn't necessarily a good idea: it always seemed to be raining, the music was deafening, and some people, who had travelled a long way from home, got separated from their friends. The bad-trip tent was kept busy. But there were two authentic hippies, Neb and George, who could always deal with any adverse drug reaction. For Neb and George the hippy credo of love and peace represented a self-evident truth. Their hair was waist-length, they had multi-coloured flowing clothes and sandals made from motor-cycle tyres. They were uncritical and accepting of others, and bad trips became funny, wondrous experiences as they caressed, cuddled and joked with young people who, moments before, had been terrified. Everyone learnt from them, and because of them it was hardly ever necessary for the doctors to give any medication.

CHAPTER 8

Love in Idleness

One of the people who was made uneasy by my frequent absences from home was Edith, our latest au pair. After a summer holiday when I joined Mel in Majorca for a week, leaving her with George and the children in Wales, she gave in her notice. As Tom and Candy were now eight and ten I thought they needed more grown-up company. I put the following advert in the *New Statesman*: 'Together couple wanted to be around when school-age children come home. S/c 2-room flat with own kitchen. Sounds provided.' The words 'together' and 'sounds' were the cultural key: it meant they could smoke dope, but not so much as to make them irresponsible.

I was inundated with letters. One was from Martin Amis who described himself as a young writer needing somewhere to live and work while he finished his first novel. In Amis's autobiography he describes the squalid room he was living in at the time, but not his failed application to supervise Tom and Candy's homework. Out of all the letters I chose Jo and

John to interview, probably because they were the only couple to reply. Jo told me later that she had taken two days to compose the letter which she wrote, very stoned, sitting on the floor and using the sleeve cover of a Jefferson Airplane LP to lean on.

We met in a pub in Camden Town. I had no shoes on and was wearing a long pink satin nightdress from Biba. Biba was a shop in Kensington for fashion-conscious thin girls with very little money. The entrance was magical, with curved mirrors and walls painted dark purple; narrow, black velvet-covered stairs led to the communal dressing room; clothes were not hung on rails but draped over hat stands. There were no bright colours; knee-length boots were dusky pinks and mauves.

John and Jo were sitting outside the pub in the September sun when I arrived. John was tall, with shoulder-length, black, very straight, clean hair. Jo looked more conventional in jeans and a T-shirt, and although she wasn't at all pretty she had a mobile, generous-looking face and was very motherly to John, who didn't speak at all. We all got on and three weeks later they moved in.

I stayed in their first evening. John cooked lasagne for themselves and the children, and invited me up to join them. I was astonished – no one had ever cooked for me in my own home before.

They made my life much easier and I no longer felt so guilty spending long days at Release. I was also able to do the late nights there – twice a week we stayed open until ten o'clock. But another reason why life was easier was that I had an ally in our new office manager, Eileen.

Eileen had been a simultaneous translator at the UN. She spoke several languages and was studying to be a solicitor. She was tall, blonde, beautiful and very clever, not a hippy, and sided with me in bringing a little more structure to the organisation. Her husband George was a hospital doctor, but we didn't see much of him as he soon disappeared in India and later emerged under another name as the Bhagwan's doctor. The Bhagwan was an Indian guru who had a fleet of white Rolls Royces. He always sniffed his disciples (and there were many) when they came to him for an audience as he didn't like them to use any soap or scent. They were dressed in orange and the favoured (and again there were many) had sex with him.

We also had a new helper in Jeremy. Jeremy was a sociologist and had been recruited to write a report on Release. This report, if favourable, was to be used for raising more funds from charitable trusts. Jeremy had a bony elegance and dark mournful blue eyes. He and Eileen had a brief affair and the next time I took the children to Wales they came too. Jo and John also came, but not George, who had gone to Patmos with his new aristocratic girlfriend, Venetia.

Venetia was tall, elegant and had rich and titled lovers who gave her jewels and holidays. George didn't do the jewels, but she loved art as much as George did and they went to art galleries, restaurants and the cinema together. George was proud to have such a long-legged, expensive-looking mistress who was not only very witty but had the androgynous looks that he admired in women – and men. Venetia was proud to have a bohemian intellectual lover. She was still able to maintain her relationship with her most established lover as he was married and could not insist on total fidelity. However, he didn't like it when he once found George in Venetia's bed.

One night the lover, very drunk, telephoned and announced that he was coming round. Venetia in a dignified manner said that it wasn't convenient. But earlier that evening Venetia and George, arriving back from an erotic film festival in Frankfurt and struggling with their luggage in the rain, had left the key in the lock. The lover entered noisily and Venetia jumped out of bed and endeavoured to prevent him from entering the bedroom. He pushed past her and saw George on his hands and knees searching for his socks under a chair. 'Who the hell are you?' he demanded. 'I'm George Melly,' was the reply. 'Well, you've got a face like a toad,' said the lover and, getting undressed, added, 'This is my bed, I paid for it and I'm getting in.' George was still writing the balloons for *Flook*, the strip cartoon in the *Mail* and, as he was late delivering his script, he retired to the sitting-room and got on with his writing. When the argument in the bedroom went quiet, George retrieved his hat and rode home on his moped.

WE STILL GAVE occasional dinner parties and George wanted me to invite Venetia. I resisted. When I had worked in Mary Quant's Chelsea shop in the late 1950s, Venetia had been a customer. I knew that, apart from George, we had little in common. She told him that she remembered me from the shop as someone who was always crying.

Although our 'open' marriage was never discussed, I knew that George liked it. Even before Venetia came along, George had had quite a few girlfriends. This meant that both sides of his complicated character were satisfied: the conservative, loyal side that hated any kind of change or disorder, and the promiscuous side. He could now indulge the latter without endangering the former. I was more of a fantasist, and, as I had encouraged Mel to believe that I would one day live with him, he began to put pressure on me to name the day. But since the arrival of John and Jo, life at home was more pleasant. If George was out I often spent the evenings with them, listening to records, smoking joints, enjoying John's cooking and learning to play bridge. I pretended to Mel that I was needed to help with homework.

I hadn't yet learnt to deal with any problem except by running away and so I booked a flight to New York. There was another reason for this trip. One of the Release trustees had suggested that I might be able to get us a grant from the Ford Foundation, so, having arranged a meeting with Ford's charitable trust director, I packed all the relevant Release documents into my luggage.

The night before I left, John cooked a special meal and invited Jeremy, who had broken up with Eileen. Like John, Jeremy hardly ever spoke, but Jo and I made up for it and discussed how Tom and Candy could be kept occupied and happy while I was away. Tom was always equable but Candy, entering puberty, was often distressed. She had shaved her arms and legs and the soft fuzz had come back rather stubby. Also she and her best friend had been caught shop-lifting candles and a tablecloth. They were making a home in a disused shed.

Jo told me not to worry, and Jeremy, reclining on a large floor cushion, gazed at me the way he used to gaze at Eileen. Our rather stiff Victorian sofas and chairs had recently given way to various cushions covered in ethnic materials. I was still supple enough to sprawl satisfactorily; George didn't find it so easy, so one chair was retained for his use.

That night I slept with Jeremy, which meant there was certainly no way of going back to Mel.

I came back from New York successful. The Ford Foundation had agreed to a donation of $4,000. In return they wanted me to write a comparative study of the different ways in which the US and the UK treated their heroin addicts. I kept half the money to use for the research, which would mean returning to the States and visiting rehab centres, clinics, lawyers and doctors. As soon as I was back, Jeremy and I embarked on an affair and I hoped that, as he was a sociologist, he would come to the States with me and help write the study. Although he was ten years younger than I was, he wasn't quite Max all over again (whom I hadn't seen since the night in Weybridge). Jeremy was moody, often morose and hard to please: Eileen had sensibly extricated herself quite quickly. I might have done the same, had it not been for a weekend at the cottage and my first acid trip.

John and Jo, with Jeremy, had gone to the cottage for Christmas and I was going to join them with Tom and Candy once family obligations had been fulfilled; Patrick was staying in London with friends. We went to Andrée's on Christmas Day. Granny Maudie, her brother, Uncle Alan, George and Andrée's brother Bill and his wife Tizzy and their three children made it seem like a normal happy family. I couldn't wait to get away.

It was New Year's Eve when we arrived at the cottage and Jo told me that once the children were in bed we could do some acid.

George often reminded me that unstable people like me could go off their heads after a trip, and I had always been frightened of it. I took it anyway and the only bad thing that happened was that, like Titania under the spell of 'Love in Idleness', I fell for Jeremy, an unsuitable person.

New Year's Day was sunny and warm. We drove to the sea and when we all – Tom and Candy too – took off our clothes and swam in the freezing water, I thought I had never felt so free or been so happy.

Jeremy's flat share had come to an end and I found him a room immediately opposite our house. Our bedroom windows faced each other. My window had a Venetian blind that I could spy through; Jeremy's more sparsely furnished room had an old Indian bedspread nailed across the window. He quickly established control and said that I could only come over if a corner of the bedspread was hooked back. He didn't have a telephone, and even if mobiles had been around, his would always have been switched off.

Sometimes Tom and Candy were taken by George and Venetia to stay with friends of hers in the country. On one of these weekends I knew I was going to have the house to myself as Jo and John were also going away.

Jeremy's bedspread was firmly 'shut', but I went over anyway to tell him I was free and to make plans. It was a warm March day, the spring flowers were out and I was thinking of a picnic on Hampstead Heath. He looked at me coldly and said, 'Don't be silly, I'm spending the weekend with Eileen.'

The house felt more than empty and when I got up to pee I moved very quietly as if any noise would be too alarming. All I could hear was my heart beating loudly. I got a kitchen knife and made a rather jagged cut on my chest, it wasn't deep and I didn't bleed much. With the help of some sleeping pills I slept most of Sunday and when I got up in the early evening and looked across at Jeremy's window I saw the little square of light signalling for me to come over.

Eileen, unaware of the games Jeremy played, was in the

room with him. She was sitting, as she always did, on the floor with her long legs tucked up and her chin resting on her knees. As usual a triangle of white knickers was showing. She hadn't realised I was in love with Jeremy and told me not to mind about them going away together, that in these days of women's lib, jealousy was unnecessary, she wasn't 'back' with Jeremy, she just wanted him now and then.

I would always have been jealous, but the side effects of the acid had left me more vulnerable than usual and I was desperately unhappy. Having to hide all these feelings and pretend to be as liberated as Eileen was beyond me. I envied George, who always said he couldn't understand sexual jealousy.

There was another problem that spring. Patrick's school had been raided by the police who suspected that they would find drugs. The teachers had been made to sit in a room with the children and everyone had to put their hands on their heads. Teenage diaries had been confiscated along with aspirins and contraceptive pills. In the end nobody was charged with anything, but a boy and a girl of fourteen who refused to stop sleeping together were asked to leave. These two children had their fees paid by the local authority and therefore the school had no option but to insist on the law being upheld. Patrick said he would not stay at a school where pupils were expelled and he left to join a squat in London. George lent him some money and he set up his own business doing electrical work and started training as a computer programmer. That much we knew – what we didn't know was that he had started using heroin.

Tom had always wanted to go away to school and he

went to Monkton Wylde just before Patrick left. Candy didn't want to go to boarding school. At that time she was more conventional than Tom or Patrick, and I persuaded her to try St Christopher's just for half a term, rather than the unconventional Monkton Wylde. St Christopher's was a Quaker, vegetarian, co-educational school with a liberal atmosphere. She cried a lot when I insisted that she must go, but I promised that she need not return after half-term unless she wanted to.

As soon as they were settled at their respective schools – and Candy liked St Christopher's immediately – Jeremy and I went to America to research the drug study for Ford.

Spending our days with heroin addicts and the over-worked and underpaid people who were trying to help them was often depressing. Equally depressing was Jeremy's growing distaste for me. He would sometimes stay sleeping in the car rather than come with me as I wandered round a Release-style centre, notebook in hand, trying to think of intelligent questions. I was glad that at least Release got $2,000 and finally Jeremy wrote the report for Ford.

CHAPTER 9

Moving

Although the Severn Bridge made the journey to Wales much shorter, it was still a six- or seven-hour drive and neither George nor I now wanted to spend the holidays there *en famille*. We decided that we should sell the cottage and I should find somewhere nearer to London. And although George loved our Camden Town house it didn't suit our increasingly separate lives. I wanted my own bedroom and, although George didn't, he saw that we would have to buy somewhere cheaper in London if our country place was to be more accessible.

Our sensible four-door saloon car had been exchanged for the small camper van that I needed for pop festivals. When parked, the roof could be raised and two bunk beds unfolded. Down below, a double bed was formed out of the table and the benches. It had a tiny fridge, a sink and a double gas hob. The curtains were bright yellow and the benches were covered in orange. I bought a lot of purple plastic mugs and plates. I liked it being in such bad taste. It reminded me

of the beach hut in Essex where my brother and I had played
as children.

The van would be my home while I house-hunted for the
gothic vicarage with fishing that George wanted. Of course
I hoped that Jeremy would accompany me and then these
expeditions would be romantic as well as fruitful. I would
have been better off with a dog. Much better. Jeremy was
once persuaded to come, but he had one of his black moods
and lay with his face to the side of the van while I drove
through Gloucestershire to the Welsh borders. Otherwise I
searched by myself. George was very busy: as well as his job
as a film critic he had his own chat show and was also starting
to sing again. A few of the old jazz musicians met every
Sunday in a King's Cross pub and George was more than
happy to join them. Lunches and dinners with Venetia took
up the rest of his time.

My search became desperate, not only because I was
lonely (and sometimes frightened) sleeping in a lay-by or in
the woods by myself, but also because I couldn't find
anywhere suitable.

Anxious as I was to find a new place, the description of a
twelfth-century, falling-down tower in the Brecon Beacons
didn't make it sound worth looking at. But the friend who
had sent me the particulars and had seen the Tower said that
it was unique, near a famous trout river, and that I should at
least go and see it.

The local estate agent said he would meet me at the
station. I didn't have the van because a staff member of
Release was using it to take all the Release paraphernalia to a
pop festival in Devon.

On the train I snorted some coke in the toilet and then smoked a joint to calm down. I stumbled off the train without my shoes and dropped several magazines on to the line. The estate agent, whose name was Simon, probably thought he was making a wasted journey. He didn't necessarily change his mind when I pushed open the heavy oak door of the Tower and without looking inside, said, 'I'll buy it.'

We went up the road to the pub and I signed a bit of paper which said I agreed to buy the Tower for £14,800 and then I crossed over the road and started hitching to the pop festival in Devon. It wasn't so much that I had fallen in love with the Tower – although I did later – but that I was thoroughly fed up with the search. Simon told me later, when we became friends, that he was so disenchanted by the experience that he chucked in the job and became a sheep farmer.

The Tower had one large ground-floor room which had been divided with a lath-and-plaster partition. In one corner were some winding stone steps that, half-way up, were filled in with cement and rubble. Inside the front door were some rickety wooden stairs which had replaced the stone ones and led up to the first floor. Here another enormous room was also divided down the middle, stopping just short of a blocked-up, south-facing, medieval window. Obviously the people who had lived there since the twelfth century had no time to stare at the views and had simply been concerned with not letting heat escape from ill-fitting windows.

But the views were sensational: to the south an oxbow lake where kingfishers had their nests; beyond it were fields where sheep and cattle grazed; in the distance was the river Usk and the Brecon Beacons. To the east were the remains of the moat which had once surrounded the Tower and to the west was a beautifully shaped, benign tree, which was often framed by glorious sunsets.

It wasn't the oldest building in Wales, but it was said to be the oldest inhabited one. Its last inhabitant had been the eighty-year-old widow of the river bailiff, but because she had to fetch water from the pump and there was no electricity, her family had insisted that she move to a little cottage in the town. We heard that she missed the Tower, and perhaps not only because she had lived there all her married life but because it was a house with a magic atmosphere.

In London our move was less successful. Our new home was a maisonette on three floors overlooking Parliament Hill. On the first floor was the kitchen, George's bedroom, bathroom and his sitting-room. This last room was 'done' by Venetia, who had lately become quite successful as an interior decorator. His sitting-room became a cool 1930s room with pale pink sofas and armchairs covered in sharp green linen. A beautiful butterfly-shaped mirror was hung between the windows and George's famous Magrittes covered the walls. Tom and Candy had a room each one floor up and I had two loft rooms above them. In one was a water bed and the other had the floor cushions. I stuck a crescent moon and some stars on the ceilings. After the first Christmas the fairy lights were left up, and to make my rooms inter-connect one of the conventional doors was sealed off and a mushroom-shaped hole was cut in the wall, just large enough to crawl through.

Jo and John had not moved to Parliament Hill with us, but as Jo was now working as George's secretary I still saw a lot of them both. With Jeremy we planned to drive through Yugoslavia in the van. Elaborate arrangements were made. The four of us would have two weeks on our own while Tom and Candy were still at school and then Jo and John would fly back and put the children on a plane to join me for their summer holiday.

The omens weren't good. One weekend Jeremy and I went to Chichester to see Peter Eyre, who was acting Constantine in *The Seagull*. When the curtain came down for the interval Jeremy got up without a word and disappeared. He didn't come back for the second half and I had no idea where he was. I sat miserably in my seat until Peter shot himself and then, instead of going back-stage to congratulate him, I went looking for Jeremy. He was stretched out in the back of the camper van and didn't stir until I pulled up outside his door. 'I hate that sort of thing,' he said and he got out.

Three weeks later, the day before we left for the ferry, Jeremy announced that he wasn't coming. We drove through Belgium, Germany and Austria with John at the wheel and Jo trying to choose music tapes that wouldn't remind me of Jeremy and make me cry even more. One night, when no doubt they couldn't stand the sound of me sobbing in the bunk above their heads they pulled me down to their bed. The comfort of sex and affection made it possible for me to stop moaning and wrecking their holiday.

After they left for England I had two days on my own before the children joined me. Max came with them. After the night when George confessed his love I hadn't seen him for at least a year but he'd got over his embarrassment and lately he'd begun dropping in if he was in our area. When John and Jo arrived back in London they bumped into him in Camden Market and suggested that he should come out with the children. We had a very happy time and Tom and Candy, who made us 'sleep in the tent' so that they could have the van, were thrilled: they didn't like Jeremy much and Max was fun for them to be with. We all swam and fished and made fires to cook on. But I still wanted Jeremy. He had sent two postcards to me which I had collected from the post office in Dubrovnik. One just said, 'Missing you, I'm afraid.' Unfortunately, he was waiting for me when I got back.

CHAPTER 10

Travelling

George's love affairs were not without complications either. Whenever he thought that Venetia was becoming a threat to his marriage, he started an affair to run alongside the main one. This extra affair in 1973 was with a woman as different from Venetia as it was possible to be. Venetia was upper-class, with a Mitford-style wit, while Heather was tiny, with perky breasts, platinum blonde hair, a raucous laugh and a sexy Cockney accent. Her job was delivering building materials and she drove a white van. George was happy: Venetia was just right for literary or BBC occasions and Heather was just right for jazz clubs.

When Venetia went to hear him sing, he would dedicate 'The Lady Loves Champagne' to her. For Heather, he sang a song that his band-leader had written, 'I Like a Girl who Drinks'. If I was there he would sing 'Dr Jazz' and while pointing at me would insert the line 'Who dropped the Benzedrine in Mrs Melly's Ovaltine?' If Jeremy was with me he sang 'My Blue Heaven' and altered the line 'and baby makes three' to 'and the lover makes three, we're so happy in my blue heaven'. Jeremy hated being singled out. I liked it, but I preferred 'I'm gonna sit right down and write myself a letter and make believe it comes from YOU'. His finger never faltered.

I was not so happy. Patrick didn't often come to our house but when he did, he usually chose a time when I would be out. He remained close to Candy and Tom, and to George too, but his behaviour was becoming more and more erratic and his requests for money more frequent. We were still unaware of his heroin addiction. Candy's adolescence took the predictable turn of finding me, not unreasonably, a huge embarrassment. I was not forgiven for sitting on the floor at a school meeting, even though all the chairs were occupied. Tom was more or less OK, but had enthusiastically experimented with matches and set fire to the school's games hut. The school was not insured against pyromaniacs and we had to foot the bill for rebuilding.

And Jeremy. He kept me on a loose lead, calling me to heel when it looked as if I could break free and then mocking me for my middle-class position, my extravagance, my droopy breasts and the stretch marks on my stomach. I would run whining to Jo and John and also to George. George was mystified by such masochistic behaviour and quite untouched by Jeremy's supposed charm. 'Why can't you just have fun with him?' he would say, and take me out to supper with Venetia.

There was also Release, and there I had a new friend, Penelope Tree. She had been a model, discovered when she was sixteen, first by Richard Avedon, then by David Bailey.

She looked like something wonderful from outer space and her startling appearance made her an icon of the 1960s.

She had been busted when a man who sold her some grass shopped her to the police and shortly afterwards she joined the Release staff. That autumn she discovered that David Bailey, with whom she was living, had left her and she moved out of his house near Primrose Hill and into a friend's flat. At Christmas she went to New York to her mother's house. Before she left we decided that if things got any worse with Jeremy I would join her there and we would drive across to California. Of course they did get worse, and, although he tried to shorten the lead once he knew I was going, I'd already booked my ticket.

In 1973 I arrived in New York on a freezing January day. Marietta, Penelope's mother, lived in a large brownstone house near the park on 79th Street. She was a formidable woman: I was frightened of her and so was Penelope. When she walked in to Penelope's bedroom and saw us sitting on the floor rolling joints and giggling, we both trembled at her look of disdain. One night Penelope went out to see a friend and as I went up to bed Marietta gave me her other daughter's book to read. This was *Fire in the Lake* by Frankie Fitzgerald, a history of the Vietnam War. Unfortunately, I found *Valley of the Dolls* by my bed and was discovered reading it when Marietta came up to see if I had everything I needed. Marietta had been the mistress of Adlai Stevenson and was the USA representative to the UN. She was not given to reading block-busters.

We set off in the direction of Washington in our hired car and although Penelope couldn't drive, was too shy to book a motel room, couldn't do up her safety belt and couldn't understand maps, I enjoyed feeling superior and anyway her company made up for her failings. It was some time before we managed to find our way out of New York and after driving for a couple of hours in a rain storm we realised we were lost. The freeway disappeared and the minor road that we found ourselves on petered out at what looked like a nuclear power station.

Mrs Perfect had packed a torch and we got out to map-read. I thought I could see where we had gone wrong, but when we got back into the car, it wouldn't start. I always reacted to this kind of potential major disaster more effectively than to minor ones, like George burning my paper knickers. I lifted the bonnet and stared at the engine. Nothing obvious was wrong but the key would not turn the motor. After an hour of this I was beginning to wonder if we'd have to sleep in the car and wait till our hosts in Washington organised a police hunt. We got back in and I said that we should do everything in the same order as when we started off. Penelope made a wild swooping movement with her seat belt and it stuck half way. I got out and strapped her in and then did my own belt up. The engine roared happily: without our belts the car was immobilised.

After Washington we drove through Virginia, Tennessee and Mississippi to New Orleans. Another potential flaw in Penelope as a travelling companion emerged when it became apparent that she couldn't stand Country and Western music. I loved it, but she gave such yelps of pain as she progressed through all the local radio stations, finding nothing but Dolly Parton or Hank Williams, that I kept my mouth shut and let her struggle with the tape recorder. Nothing mechanical ever worked for her: she would open her cassette case and all the tapes would fall on to the floor; when inserted, the tape would stick, spew out its contents, and she would give up. We drove happily in silence, as the one thing she could do was roll a joint. Although I was just as stoned, I was a lot older and far less paranoid, so I was the one to book the room and organise supper. Penelope would follow, dropping her cassettes, her clothes and her books as we found ourselves in another identical motel room.

After the long, dusty road that runs through Texas, it was a relief to reach New Mexico and Arizona. In Texas we had found ourselves crossing the border into Mexico and then panicked about coming back in. Bringing grass into the States from Mexico was a serious crime, but the border police were too busy inspecting the Mexicans' papers to bother with us. Also the Texan men seemed to resent a woman driver. They would drive along beside us, staring down from their huge trucks, and then, having overtaken us, would slow down to twenty miles an hour, not allowing us to pass.

We spent a night at the Grand Canyon and before arriving in Las Vegas explored the Painted Desert. After that, Las Vegas was a shock. There were fruit machines in the toilets, gambling tables surrounded by predatory-looking people, and a very fat Elvis Presley in a white satin suit. He came on to the stage puffing and sweating but before he'd finished his first number a woman had fainted at my feet. By the time I'd hauled her outside, found a medic and located her friends, Elvis was doing his last encore.

Five weeks after leaving New York we arrived in San Francisco where we were staying with Brian Rohan, a lawyer I'd met while researching the report for the Ford Foundation. He had taken me to a small club where a relatively unknown Bette Midler was performing. This time he went one better, and on our last night got us tickets for our hero, Bob Dylan, who was singing at Winterland.

Waiting for us at his house were letters from George and Jeremy, and for Penelope an invitation to join some friends on a small sailing boat. George had written that he was making a record with his band, and Jo wrote that she and John had decided to move to America although not until the spring.

Jeremy had written, 'Although you are many miles away, I don't feel very separate from you. . . . It's hard being without you.'

CHAPTER 11

From the Usk to the Teardrop Isle

I was back for the February half-term and I went to the
Tower with the children. We had employed a local
architect who was drawing up plans to restore the Tower and
turn it into a more habitable building. It needed a new roof.
The winding stone stairs needed to be cleared of the rubble,
re-built and made safe. The loft above was to be turned into
a bedroom. Somehow a bathroom would be 'hung' between
the two floors; as the ceilings were high this would be quite
easy. Eventually water and electricity would be laid on.
Meanwhile we would live as the previous occupant had
done: drawing water from the pump, lighting candles and oil
lamps, gathering wood for the open fires and never washing.
I slept with the children in one bed for warmth and we were
only disturbed when Blackie, our cat, would drop a headless
mouse on our pillow.

The architect explained that because it was a listed
building it would take at least eighteen months before any
work could begin. Rather than leave our furniture in store we

moved it all in. The farmer said that when the building work eventually started and we had to move the furniture out again, we could use his barns for storing it. As a lot of our furniture had been made before electric light was invented, it looked quite at home.

When the Tower was built in the twelfth century it was the stone keep to a wooden castle. A couple of centuries later, when defending the Welsh borders was no longer an issue and the castle had fallen down, the Tower became a domestic dwelling place. Because it was a humble building, the exact dates and its military use are obscure. I often tried to find out more. There were wonderful rumours of an underground passage leading from a cellar (which we never found) to Pencelli castle on the other side of the river, but the only certain thing I discovered was its connection to the poet Henry Vaughan, known as the Swan of Usk. Vaughan had lived in Holly Bush Cottage two hundred metres away across a field and his cousin had lived in the Tower. The cousin was Vaughan's accountant; perhaps the poet visited our house and wrote 'I saw eternity the other night' while sitting in the living-room and taking a break from his finances. Two holly bushes mark the spot where Vaughan's cottage was, and his river, the Usk, was where George was going to fish.

George didn't come much that spring. He was often with Venetia and they both liked a degree of comfort and at least some hot water to wash in. Playing at 'making house' was not fun for them, but for me it was one of the happiest times.

One weekend Jeremy came down. He was working with a friend building film sets and saving up to travel. He told me that he was going to Sri Lanka, 'the teardrop island', and would like me to go with him. He said that if we were alone, dependent on each other and I didn't have my 'props', we could be happy together. We planned that he would leave in early April and I would follow after the Easter holidays. George would have the children for the May half-term and they would fly out to join me in July. I would then come back with them for the beginning of the autumn term. Jeremy was getting a one-way ticket and didn't say where he would be going in September.

The positive side of being a control freak is being an efficient organiser. To leave George in good hands was relatively easy. He had a secretary, three girlfriends, a daily, and I stocked the freezer. The plans for the Tower were complete and about to be submitted to the interested parties. They would not be sent out to tender until after I was back. I was flying with Aeroflot, the Russian airline; so were Tom and Candy. A night in Moscow meant visas had to be obtained and they would travel as unaccompanied children. I made lists of lists: explain dishwasher, check chemist list, cotton swimsuit, books. I travelled to Sri Lanka with all twelve volumes of Proust. Somehow they never got read.

Within a week of Jeremy arriving in Colombo he was sending me letters requesting other items to add to my rucksack: film, a tripod, batteries, etc. He also quoted John Masters, 'This valley was to be our Eden.'

In the south of the country is a mountain called Adam's Peak and Sri Lanka had other claims to being the origin of the Garden of Eden. It was beautiful and diverse: there were jungles, wet and dry, waterfalls, coral reefs, sandy beaches, exotic fruit, leopards, elephants and an ancient civilisation. This didn't prevent the bitter civil war between the Tamils in the north and the Sinhalese in the south; nor did Jeremy and I last long in the garden.

By the time the children came out I was mostly on my own and learning to live without my 'props'. Sometimes Jeremy would appear and we would travel together for a short while and then he would disappear again to the other side of the island.

I was trying to write a novel based on my early life and had been given an advance by a publisher. This had paid for my ticket, but I was finding writing very difficult. The evenings, when I felt most lonely, would have been the ideal time, but since I was on the Equator, the sun went down at 6.15 and it was dark. Sometimes a rest house would have a little electric light and there were always candles. Hurricane and paraffin lamps attracted insects the size of sparrows, so usually I would just re-read my letters from home and go to bed at 8.30. George wrote often. He described a smart dinner party that he and Venetia had given in our house. Jo and John had offered to come round to cook for it but they smoked so much hash and got so stoned that it was midnight before any food appeared. He told me that his record *Son of Nuts* had been such a success that the producer was thinking of putting him on in New York, that he had a contract for a book about his naval days, and was often on television. But he always ended the letter 'Come back soon to your fat and fairly famous husband.'

The news of Patrick was good too. He had cashed in the one-way ticket to Australia that George had bought him and had gone to live in Paris instead. The week before he should have left for Oz, he joined a company called 'Le Grand Magic Circus', who had been performing in London. The Magic Circus was a group of young French actors, and their show was wild, anarchic and fun. Patrick was in his element: he was in charge of the lighting and the fireworks. He loved Paris, where he rented his own little flat and he now spoke French fluently. I had longed for him to be on the other side of the world, but I had dreaded it too. France seemed the perfect solution.

I sat on some rocks by a lake covered in giant water-lilies reading the letter about Patrick. George wrote that he was hoping to go over to Paris with Heather and see the show. I felt very sorry for myself and wished that I was going too. On the other hand I didn't envy him his invitation to No. 10. He and Venetia had been invited by Harold Wilson, then prime minister, to dine with the Canadian Ambassador and other luminaries.

Sometimes George would write that he had sent me a parcel and I would travel across the country to the post office in Colombo. I was spending most of my time on the other side of the island which was much more primitive. Colombo, which looked so ramshackle when I first arrived, now seemed the height of sophistication. I would treat myself to a night in the air-conditioned hotel, buy an English paper, and sometimes read about George.

After the children arrived I hired a car and we became proper tourists, visiting the game parks, tea plantations and ancient cities. It was too soon to count the hours before 14 September when our flights were booked, but I counted the days. So did Tom and Candy.

Jeremy came to see us off. He too was leaving the island and going on to Australia. I was still in love with him, but I had just enough sense to know that it was a barren match. I also knew that he feared me, that he needed to put himself on the other side of the world, as far away from me as possible, not just because he feared me, despised and belittled me, but because he loved me.

If Colombo had seemed like a huge city after the East Coast, London appeared ugly and vast. George met us at the airport. My relief at being home was tempered by knowing that I had made a fool of myself: I had been in one of the most beautiful countries in the world and I had wasted that experience; I had been among people many of whom were poor, and some who didn't have enough to eat, and I had allowed self-pity to overwhelm me.

We drove home through the depressing suburbs of West London. George was full of his own news and career and the children found it hard to get a word in. Tom wanted to describe falling into a giant ants' nest. Candy wanted to tell him about Josie, our pet monkey. Much to my dismay, our Tamil driver had separated the baby monkey from its family and given it to us. Candy had become its surrogate mother, and the two of them would lie on the veranda comforting each other, the monkey gazing up at the tree-tops where other monkeys played, and Candy dreaming of friends and TV.

The school term started and the children left. I tried to adapt to London life. But my experience of a Third World culture, however superficial, made me want to live differently. The amount of rubbish and waste we accumulated in London was distressing. I would only eat curry – without a knife and fork. I slept on the floor and I slept all the time. George's patience was severely tried, but he staggered up to my room with trays of food, a bottle of wine and Valium – two little yellow pills on a pretty saucer. If Jo and John had still been there I might, with their help, have pulled myself together, but they had gone to live in San Francisco.

A few weeks after I was back, a young man turned up to paint the kitchen. George was pleased for two reasons, he wanted the kitchen done and he thought the young man was a girl. Billy had a gentle face, shoulder-length blond hair and lots of silver jewellery. 'Gold is vulgar,' he used to say.

At the end of his first day's painting I offered to drive Billy home. I thought that on the way I could carefully explain that perhaps painting wasn't quite his thing. He hadn't used any dust sheets and there was more paint on the floor than on the walls. The brushes had been left to soak in my best saucepan and the cat had left painted paw marks up the stairs.

The problem was that Billy didn't have a home. He had the offer of floor space in one squat, but his friends were out. At the second place a waif-like girl came to the door shaking her head and muttering 'heavy scene, man'. Billy didn't appear surprised when I offered him my floor space: hippies had their faults but they were not possessive about their 'space' – or their belongings. I made some hot chocolate and toast, but when I carried it up, Billy was fast asleep in my bed and wearing my satin Biba nightdress.

CHAPTER 12

The Rescuer and the Baby Snatcher

The next morning we went back to Billy's most recent squat to collect his belongings. These included two goldfish called David and Bowie.

Billy's teenage years had not been easy. His parents were conventional and Billy was not. He had been asked to leave two public schools and on holiday in Israel had taken acid while listening to Leonard Cohen. This was not a happy experience and it had left him insecure, vulnerable and paranoid. But his qualities – lack of guile, sweetness and charm – made everyone want to help him. George called him Candide. He hated saying 'no' to anything he was asked for. 'Have you seen my book, got any matches, peeled the potatoes?' Billy would reply, 'Not really.'

Nobody seemed to find it odd that I had a boyfriend of seventeen. I hadn't asked him his age, but one day when he made a particularly naïve remark, Penelope asked him and he replied, 'I'll be eighteen next week,' and George, who was relieved that Jeremy was safely off in Australia, took us all to the Hard Rock Café for Billy's birthday.

We stayed in a lot. Billy had no interest in the cinema, dinner parties or the theatre. He helped me shop and cook and when Tom and Candy came back for Christmas he spent a lot of time with them watching television and listening to music.

Before Billy, Christmas had always been something to get through, but Billy bought a huge tree (unfortunately too tall for our ceilings), spent a fortune on sparkling decorations and made everyone a stocking. On Christmas Eve we all went to the midnight service at St Martin-in-the-Fields.

Granny Maudie and her brother Uncle Alan, who was gay, came for Christmas lunch and they both fell in love with Billy. Fortunately Billy didn't realise that Uncle Alan's smiles and gestures of affection were sexual; Billy was frightened of homosexuals and thought that they were 'degenerate'. Granny Maudie's adoration of Billy was in marked contrast to her opinion of Venetia. Venetia was placed next to Uncle Alan, and while she politely listened to Alan's very long tales of catching a train, or a golfing dinner, Maudie could be heard muttering, 'She's getting her claws into *him* now.' Venetia was also wearing some of her best jewels. One brooch was of little diamonds forming a 'V'. Maudie became convinced that this had something to do with George. George, although always generous, was not in the habit of buying diamonds.

When the holidays were over, Billy and I went down to the Tower. The builders had not started work; the local council and also the committees in charge of listed buildings had to pass the plans and it was taking ages. Luckily the Tower was only listed as Grade 2 so we were allowed to make changes to the inside.

But Billy had the capacity to make everything seem fun, so although we were still without the basic services, he chopped wood, fetched water and, with an enormous scythe, began to clear the garden.

George was going to New York to sing and was then planning an early spring holiday with Venetia in Morocco. Billy and I started to plan one too. We would drive through Spain in the van and then take the ferry to Casablanca. To finance the trip I rented out my two rooms, cashed in a life insurance policy and bought some Frisbees which we intended to sell in campsites and on the beaches. We would spend six weeks in Morocco and end up in France. The journalist Dee Wells, Freddie Ayer's wife, was going to lend us her cottage near Toulon, where we would spend Easter with Tom and Candy. They were to fly out to join us as unaccompanied children.

The journey across Spain was beautiful, but Billy was desperate. He couldn't drive, he didn't read and he didn't like the way the Spanish shop-keepers looked at him when we stopped for provisions. The pre-Raphaelite hippy look had not reached the mountain villages of central Spain. Amongst nineteenth-century Afghan tribes or the people of Bhutan, Billy might have passed as one of them. His gold locks would have identified him as having Alexander the Great or an English Empire-builder as an ancestor, and he would not have stood out as he did here.

It wasn't hard to persuade him out of his purple velvet

trousers and satin shirt and into blue jeans. I also taught him to drive and to read. Just as some children are now born computer-literate, Billy could drive the first time he sat behind the wheel. Reading wasn't quite so easy. As well as books for myself I had brought books by authors that I thought Billy would like: Agatha Christie, Carlos Castaneda, Patricia Highsmith and Hemingway. Billy would read a page and then fling it on the floor shouting, 'This is phoney stuff.' In the case of Castaneda he was probably right. But then he picked up *One Hundred Years of Solitude* by Gabriel García Márquez and he was away. Being new to it he read quite slowly and when he had finished he started at the beginning again.

George and Venetia were due to arrive in Marrakesh about the same time as us, and when we got to the campsite there was a message from them. They were at La Mamounia Palace Hotel and would we like to meet for dinner.

I rang up and asked if, as the campsite had only minimal washing facilities, we could have a bath in their suite first.

George had just had his bath and Billy was very embarrassed when George strolled about the room with nothing on. When he also broke wind rather loudly, again it was Billy who was scarlet with embarrassment.

We stayed only a week in Marrakesh as we both wanted to go south into the desert, across the Atlas Mountains and down the coast. Also, Billy had been ripped off trying to buy some hash from a young lad who had promised to be his 'best friend'. The situation wasn't improved by Billy's remembering that I had warned him about 'best friends'. Billy had sat for two hours outside the shop into which the

best friend had entered and vanished – presumably out of
the back exit – before coming back in tears. We had sold only
six Frisbees – although Billy had given four away to children
– and we knew things would be cheaper out of the city.

All over Morocco there are campsites. Not all of them are
official. Billy and I, along with other campers in tents and
vans, would sometimes be dawn-raided and sent packing. In
spite of this we tried to avoid camping in isolation. It felt

safer to be with other people. There was also useful inform-ation to be exchanged: where there was a good beach, which vendor sold the best honey, when was market day, etc. And I liked having other people to talk to. I had to avoid talking to men because Billy was as jealous of me as I had once been of George. At least I understood his fear and his uncontrollable rages.

Tidying the van was the major morning task: beds folded away, candle wax cleaned up, dirty clothes and washing up carried to the stream, cassettes put back in boxes and ashtrays emptied. Then it would be time for my massage. Billy, whose only paid job had been working on a health farm for three weeks, was convinced he could smooth my wrinkles away. 'If I can make you look young until you're forty, that's two more years, I will be twenty, ready to get married and you will be too old to get another boyfriend – I will be your last one.'

After a trip through the Gorge du Todra and across the desert to Zagora we realised the van needed some repairs and decided to go to Agadir.

Having found a garage that would do the work we found that we were short of money again. It was Billy's idea that we should sell our King's Road cowboy boots. The man in the carpet shop summoned his friend to guide Billy to another friend who would give the 'best' price for them. I was invited to wait in the shop and drink some tea. Naively I agreed, and Billy set off. He returned an hour later in tears and without the boots, having been led a goose chase through the souks and side streets. I had also been chased around the shop, and had only just avoided rape.

Billy was very frightened and hysterical. He screamed that he didn't believe that I had resisted. He said that he couldn't go on loving someone who was fancied 'in that way'.

That night I checked us into a tourist hotel, swallowed my pride and used my credit card to pay the bill.

Billy calmed down and wrote a letter to his best friend. He often wrote letters, although he never posted them. In this one he wrote, 'I am looking at Di at the moment. Far out. She is so beautiful. She is opening my mind and being so kind and loving to me. I dig her so much.'

I also used my credit card to get the cash for the garage and two days later we set off for the mountains.

On our map we had found what looked like the perfect place to stay. And so it was: shady palm trees, a clear stream rushing straight down from the mountains, rocks to dry our clothes on and friendly children.

On the other side of the track which led down to our oasis was a small village. That night we were invited to supper at the house of a respectable-looking man of about forty. After a meal of mutton and beans he started rolling joints. When he thought we were sufficiently stoned he suggested we should exchange 'some petit souvenirs'. Neither of us were so out of our heads that we were willing to swap cassettes, torches, watches or our clothes for a broken Barbie doll, a few ancient tins of Nesquik or some spent batteries. But there was no ill feeling when we broke up for the night. On our way back to the van we were accosted by a young man who asked us if we would look at his sick daughter. She did look very sick and I offered to drive her ten miles to the nearest hospital. The offer was politely refused; but the next morning the father reappeared and said that Fatima was worse and could we go at once. Her mother and father sat in the back of the van holding the child who must have been about seven years old.

But on the way to the hospital she died, and her parents insisted that I turn the van round and take her back to their village. When we stopped, they both jumped out and ran towards their house. At first we thought they had left us with their dead child, and Billy gathered her into his arms and carried her in the direction they'd gone. But they had only gone for help and soon the whole village came running out.

Billy and I started packing up the van. Without saying anything, we knew it was time to leave Morocco. If only, I thought, I'd taken her to hospital that night; if only I hadn't taken her at all. I swallowed some speed and drove to the border. I swallowed some more and drove through Spain. The third one got us to Dee's cottage in France. Soon the children would be here.

CHAPTER 13

Weaning Billy

Dee's house in France was cold and haunted, Tom and Candy missed the TV and their friends, it rained a lot and Billy complained that I shouldn't take speed as it made me look old. Dee arrived after a few days and we all cheered up. She had a very sharp and sarcastic wit but as long as she was on your side you could remain unscathed. She wasn't universally popular and some people found her too brash, too outspoken and just occasionally too rude. Appearing on a current affairs TV programme called *Three After Six* with George in the mid-1960s, she had suggested that the police were more interested in 'kicking some poor little bugger down stairs' than finding a missing Goya that had been recently stolen. She was never invited back, and rather sadly – the programme had financed many lunches at Wheeler's – nor was George. Our neighbour, Jonathan Miller, had called the exorbitant fees that the participants received 'fairy gold', because it was disastrous to rely on such an unreliable source of income. Shirley, the producer of the programme, lived round the corner from us, and after we had been reduced to selling a small drawing by Klee, George took to hanging about in the street at the time when she usually left for work. She would greet him warmly, but the fairy gold remained elusive. Dee wasn't so worried, she had just written a bestseller called *Jane* about a woman who had got pregnant and didn't know which of her three lovers was the putative father.

We mentioned the haunting to her and, never one to let a name remain under covers, she replied, 'Everyone who stays here says that, even sensible people like Roy Jenkins.' Jenkins had been Home Secretary in the Labour government from 1965 to 1967. So sensible was he that he had reformed the abortion laws.

The drive home through France was uneventful until we got in a muddle at the petrol station and filled the van up with diesel instead of petrol. Arriving at the customs in Dover we were pulled over. It seemed as if they had been waiting for us. During a bored moment in Wales, Tom and Candy had painted the van with pink and green swirls of colour. When the customs officials questioned the children as to what was the most exciting thing they had done on holiday, Tom told them about the day at the garage when the diesel fuel had been drained. By that time, angry at not finding even the remains of a joint, they decided the drugs must be in the petrol tank. Before they could drain it I remembered I had kept the petrol receipt when I filled up at Calais. There was no way there could be room for anything else, and after three hours they let us go. Candy was very silent on the way home. She was thirteen and the customs men had read her diary aloud to each other and sniggered.

We were still waiting for the building plans of the Tower to be passed so I decided to spend the summer there and see if I could hurry things along. This was a good idea for several reasons: all the ground-floor windows had been broken – perhaps because the place seemed unoccupied; George wanted to fish but as he couldn't manage there on his own he wanted me to be there; and Billy found London 'too heavy' after Morocco.

My mother had taken some friends to the Tower while I was away and told me that she had found some small pieces of hash which she had carefully put in a bowl. When we lit the oil lamp and candles, got the fire going and fetched the water, Billy rolled up a joint with Mum's pieces of hash and settled down to watch the sunset. He pronounced it to be the best black, but I wasn't convinced. The next time I was in London, I took it to Release, who confirmed my suspicion that it was mouse droppings.

We got so used to living without the usual 'services' that it was hard to imagine how things could be improved. Emptying the Elsan was no one's favourite job, but as long as it was done before it could slop on to your feet it was OK. Also the winter was a long way off. Friends came, George fished, we swam in the river and Billy passed his driving test.

Although we often barbecued our lunch, making an evening meal was more of a sweat on the little camping stove, and once a week we went out to dinner. Billy was learning that dressing in an unconventional manner in Wales was as bad as it had been in Spain. We were refused entry at two different pubs.

That summer it became obvious that Billy would have to

get a job, and when we went back to London in October he started work as a waiter at Ronnie Scott's club.

I knew that Billy was beginning to be uncomfortable about his relationship with me. That year, 1975, I was going to be thirty-eight, and sometimes I saw him looking at me and I knew he had spotted a new wrinkle. Occasionally he suggested that I should do some exercises to stop my bottom sagging. I knew about droopy breasts, but I didn't often look at my bottom and was unaware of its sag. I wanted him to move on. I cared for him. I didn't love him (instinctively he knew that), but I knew I would miss him and I would have no one to care for. Tom and Candy didn't need me in the same way.

I had been to see Patrick in Paris and although he didn't seem well and talked about returning home, I didn't notice, or didn't want to notice how much he needed care. I dreaded him coming back to live with us and I dreaded his wild schemes for making money that reminded me of his father: I knew that he would ask George to fund them and when George would complain mildly, I would feel torn between the two of them. He was also too unhappy and underneath too fragile to ask for help. He had tried to tell me about his heroin addiction by leaving a syringe on the table in his flat, but when I questioned him, he said it was for a 'vitamin injection', and I think I believed him. He wanted me to make up for all the years when I had left him, but I couldn't – his physical presence was too large, his character too confrontational for me and anyway it was too late.

George needed me in Wales but not in London; he was busy with a new girlfriend whom he now saw nearly as often as he saw Venetia and Heather. Before George went back on the road he had sung at a pub every Sunday and there he met Patricia who was a folk singer. On the whole George despised folk singing, but Patricia had red hair and came from Liverpool. I never understood why being a Liverpudlian was considered superior to coming from any other part of England. My first husband was very snobbish and had asked me not to mention my Essex background, but at least he wouldn't have thought coming from Liverpool was any better than being an Essex girl.

Patricia was very jealous of me but for only one reason. I had taken acid and she hadn't. Nor had George and he asked me if I would make the arrangements to put this right.

The trip was carefully planned. Norman Zimberg, an American psychiatrist, had written a book called *Drugs, Set and Setting*. He wrote that the acid must be pure, the people friendly and the habitat sympathetic. My rooms with their floor cushions, fairy lights and candles were considered to be more suitable than George's conventional sitting-room; conventional, that is, except for the Magrittes.

Apart from George, Patricia, me and Billy, there was Dominic who was our supplier. I didn't trust Dominic, but he had insisted on being there and at least he was very experienced with acid.

After he had swallowed his tab, George decided that as he was hallucinating quite wildly he would like to look at his Magrittes. I led him down the green-carpeted stairs which I thought were flooded with rushing water. I stepped carefully, trying not to get my feet wet, and George looked at his Magrittes for what might have been five minutes or an hour.

He pronounced them unchanged and we went up to join the others. Patricia was sitting in the middle of the floor and weeping. Of course I should have known better than to leave her with Dominic and Billy, but when I went over to her she started to laugh and said, 'You think I'm crying because I'm having a bad trip. I'm not, it's because he gave everyone real acid except me.' Wicked Dominic then gave her some more.

At one moment during the long and ghastly night that followed, she thought she was Billie Holiday and started singing some of Billie's more tragic songs. Later, when a chink of reality returned, she couldn't remember where she had put her gold Cartier watch. A desperate search continued for the rest of the night until it was discovered by Dominic, pinned to the cork notice-board in the kitchen along with my shopping lists and reminders about ringing the plumber. Billy restored a little sanity by finding some orange juice and a huge cheese-cake which he cut into slices. 'Look,' he said, when we trooped back up with the watch, 'it's a party.'

George had avoided a 'bad trip', but he hadn't much liked it. He told me that every time he looked at me, my face aged from that of a young girl to an old woman and then turned into a skull.

Patricia went on tour in Europe the next week, and we didn't see her again. Tom and Candy were pleased; they hadn't much liked her and much preferred Venetia who reminded them of Penelope Keith in TV's *The Good Life*.

George was singing over the Christmas period at Ronnie Scott's again. He never really got over the thrill of singing at the same place as all the 'serious' musicians. Billy was still working there and making a big success of his job. The customers loved him, and so did one of the waitresses. Although he still slept in my bed, an incest-like taboo had crept up on us and we lay there like mother and son. Sometimes we had mother and son rows and I learnt, as George had learnt, that if you mother someone they may become wary of sex with you. Billy felt guilty about seeing the waitress; I felt guilty because I didn't have the courage to ask him to leave. I looked forward to the spring when I could go back to the Tower and wait for the builders to start. The plans had finally been passed, and the builders had promised to be finished by August when George would have four weeks' holiday.

CHAPTER 14

The Gypsy Camp

The long hot summer of 1976 started on 9 May, Tom's birthday. Billy and I went down to his school in Dorset and took him out mackerel fishing for the day. Afterwards I dropped Billy at the station as he was working at Ronnie Scott's that night, and drove on to the Tower.

In the early spring I had watched a pair of swans mating on the oxbow and spied on their rather untidy nest from my bedroom window. I wanted to see if their eggs had hatched. There was no sign of eggs or cygnets and the swans were just swimming around. Suddenly, one of them gave a little shake and four fluffy things were shot in to the water.

Billy had cleared the brambles and thicket from the garden so that I would have a space for the van. The roof was off the Tower and the builders had started putting the new one on. I drove into Brecon the next day and bought three tents, one big enough for two or three to sleep in, a smaller one for George and a large one that could be used as a living room. Billy and I had the van which we shared with a cat that turned up called Sheba. Almost immediately she gave birth to three kittens. We gave one away, one died, so we kept the last one and called it Desmond.

As the farmer had allowed us to store our furniture and belongings in his barns I was able to retrieve things that would make my camp more habitable. At first, thinking it would soon rain, I only got things that could either be put away easily or that wouldn't spoil if they got wet. But as the weeks went by and I woke every morning to a cloudless blue sky, I fetched more and more stuff: wicker chairs, a Victorian wash-stand with jug and basin, carpets and the floor cushions. It was heaven; I even bought a shiny new and superior Elsan.

Every evening at five o'clock the builders would knock off for the day and I would go and inspect the changes. A lot of time had been wasted excavating for the rumoured cellar with its underground passage. An eighty-year-old stone-mason from Cardiff, who had worked at the Tower in the 1920s, was brought over to help. He couldn't find it, and even if it had been discovered, apart from its historical and archaeological importance, it would have been full of water and possibly rats.

The Tower itself never flooded. It had been built on a man-made mound and had once been surrounded by a moat. Sometimes, when the river flooded, the water would come halfway up the mound and only the tops of the oak trees could be seen poking up from the meadows. But the back step never got wet.

Clearing the huge lumps of rubble from the stairs to the first floor and rebuilding the steps was a triumph. These stairs were inside the seven-foot-thick walls which over the centuries had crumbled and become dangerous. The rickety wooden staircase in the front porch that replaced them was chopped up for the bonfire. There was still a lot to do – bathroom, kitchen, loft, etc. It was already June and George's holiday was starting in six weeks. I felt responsible that he didn't have a proper bed or lavatory, but as it still hadn't rained since 9 May I retrieved a bed and a little writing table from the barn and furnished a tent for him. Camping Gaz provided him with enough light to write by. He was trying to finish his book *Rum, Bum and Concertina* about his life in the Navy.

Billy sometimes travelled down on a Sunday if he had the Monday off, but he was now seeing Sarah the waitress regularly. I was also glad that he was taking care of things at home and sometimes cooking for George. I hoped that he would move out once I came back in the winter.

Patrick also came down to the Tower. He had arrived back from Paris looking grey and thin. I had not been much help. On a few occasions when he had nowhere to sleep he had stayed with us in London. Predictably, we quarrelled: about the parking fines that he collected every time he borrowed my car, about the front door being left open. It seemed as if anything could set us off. I also quarrelled with George whose gold fob watch, which had belonged to his father, had gone missing from his bedroom cupboard. I didn't see why Patrick should be blamed when George, who was going through a very promiscuous stage, had men and women he hardly knew sometimes sharing his bed.

Though I could defend Patrick to others, I couldn't really help him; and I'm sure he must have wondered why, if I could respond to Billy's predicament, I was unable to respond to his.

But someone did respond: Kate Figes was seventeen when she met Patrick soon after his return from Paris. She was doing her A levels and she was clever, kind and beautiful. They came down to the Tower for the weekend and somehow she managed to calm things down between me and Patrick, or perhaps she just made him feel loved and happy. We picnicked in the woods, watched the goldfinch swarm on the front lawn, cooked on the bonfire and washed our hair in the river. I felt that with Kate he would be all right.

George took to the camp immediately, and, although the drought had caused the water almost to disappear, he fished in the river, banged away on his typewriter under a shady tree and rode on his new moped to the local pub every evening.

Tom and Candy were not quite so enamoured of the primitive life. With some relief I saw Tom off to Germany on a school trip. It wasn't a total success. The son of the old couple with whom he was staying had been killed in the war. The official notice of the young man's death was pinned to Tom's bedroom wall and covered in swastikas; the notice praised his dedication to the fatherland. When I met Tom off the train at Abergavenny I failed to recognise him: his hair had been cut very short and his shabby clothes replaced with a smart pale blue denim suit.

Candy had also managed to escape. Venetia had spread it around that Candy and I were not getting on. This had got back to Candy's grandfather, the painter Rodrigo Moynihan, and his second wife, Anne Dunn. They had a son, Danny, who wasn't much older than Candy. She was invited to spend the summer with them at their manor house in France. At first I had been hurt, but there was truth in what Venetia had said. Candy was now fifteen. My early behaviour when I left her father had estranged her from his side of the family, and although it was too late to make up for the lost years, she did at last have a chance to become a Moynihan and not just 'a step-pretend-Melly'.

It started raining on 31 August, but the builders had finished, the camp was dismantled, the furniture installed in the house and George went back to London. He had one more weekend at the Tower before the fishing season ended and he was bringing Venetia. The weekend wasn't without its drama. Billy had come to help me put furniture in place, and while he turned paper napkins into improbable flowers, I made lunch. Luckily it was cold trout and salad: George had lost his way (not being able to drive he had little sense of direction) and they were three hours late. George spent the next day fishing and in the evening took us all out to dinner. It was an uncomfortable occasion. George had strained his back while casting and was also becoming quite deaf. He was sitting opposite Venetia who was talking rather quietly, possibly on purpose. Every time she spoke he would have to lean forward to catch what she said, this simple movement making him give a loud yelp of pain. And Venetia didn't much like the food – 'I've chosen badly again!' she would cry in a tone that managed to combine both pleasure and disappointment as each new course was put in front of her.

The three of them went back to London the next day and

I had the house, the garden, Sheba and her kitten Desmond, to myself again. The garden had begun to take up a lot of time. In the spring I had sown and planted lots of vegetables; it was time to harvest the tomatoes, the only things to have survived the drought. In the evening I read my bible, a book called *Learning to Live in the Country*. It was full of useful tips such as how to turn old bits of lino in to firelighters, and I wondered how I was going to feel when I saw Jeremy, who had just arrived back in London from Australia.

CHAPTER 15

Mrs Perfect Polishes her Halo (and drops it)

In 1972 Sonia Orwell, George's widow, had introduced me to the writer Jean Rhys. Sonia and I had been friends since the 1960s. In some ways she was like Dee: they both found it easy to make friends and just as easy to make enemies, they were both very clever, but most of all they were both very kind and generous. In each case you had to know them well before you loved them: with Dee you had first to survive her sarcasm, with Sonia you had to put up with what could seem like snobbishness and her infatuation with anything French. I spoke not a word of the language and when Sonia had too much to drink a large part of her conversation was unintelligible to me. Orwell had married her and made her his heir and literary executor because he rightly believed she would help impoverished writers and painters. What he could not have foreseen was the way in which Sonia was cheated out of the copyright and control of the money. Naively she had trusted the man who was Orwell's acountant. She only drew a modest sum from the estate, but because of her generosity everyone assumed she was rich.

Jean Rhys was one of the many writers whom Sonia helped and probably the one who was most in need, not only of Sonia's financial aid but of the imaginative way in which she transformed Jean's life. Jean and Sonia began to correspond when Jean was living in a cold, shabby bungalow in Devon struggling to finish *Wide Sargasso Sea*, the book that was going to establish her as a great writer. Part 1 had been published in *Art and Literature*, a magazine that Sonia co-edited. Although Jean had become anxious about part of her unfinished work being made public, she warmed to the kindness shown by Sonia in her letters and when Sonia offered her a holiday in Brighton she accepted. It was a huge success: Sonia ordered flowers, champagne, clothes (which Jean loved) and even tipped the staff in advance.

From that year on, 1966, Sonia would rescue her every winter and pay for her to stay for two or three months either in a London hotel or a flat.

Following the critical acclaim of *Wide Sargasso Sea*, all Jean's books were published and, knowing how much I admired them, particularly *Voyage in the Dark* which was about Jean's life as a chorus girl and her first unhappy love affair, Sonia asked me to lunch to meet her. In 1972 Jean was over eighty. She was sitting in Sonia's pretty sitting-room wearing a soft blue dress that matched her eyes. She was so tiny and so bent and her voice was so quiet and gentle that I had to kneel at her feet to hear her. We talked about clothes and I said I would take her shopping followed by tea at the Ritz.

That winter I became one of Jean's 'helpers'. All the helpers had different roles: some could type for her, some could flirt, and some talk about writing. My role was to help her shop.

Mostly we shopped for hats and make-up, and the perfume department at Harrods was her favourite place. She had five little make-up bags which were always being sorted, although what the arrangement was meant to be I never discovered. She could never find the exact lipstick or rouge that she was looking for.

She didn't often buy a hat. Many would be tried on, but when she looked in the mirror she didn't see the person she wanted to see. It wasn't just a lost youth that was missing. Even though she had been so pretty and attractive to men and tried to make use of that, she was never happy with her looks. I once found her staring into a little hand mirror with what I thought was vanity, but she looked up at me and said, 'Found drowned.' If Peter Eyre took her out to lunch she always wanted to go to a restaurant where the lights were dim and she loved to disguise her face by painting it with his theatrical make-up. The right amount of drink could give her a little confidence, and sometimes she knew her writing was good, and that she had been able to make it 'smooth'.

At the end of the long hot summer of 1976 I went back to London and looked forward to helping with 'the Jean winter'. The hotels had begun to find her too difficult, so this year Sonia had found her a flat off Sloane Square, and Jean moved in before Christmas.

A rota of the helpers was organised: she must have someone there to give her breakfast and help her get dressed, someone to either take her some lunch, or preferably take her out, and someone to help her to bed after a light supper and then sort her pills. I loved this job; clearly I should have been a school matron. Sonia rather flatteringly said I could have run Marks & Spencer.

Of course there were problems that winter. The writer David Plante was trying to help her arrange her auto-biography which she had scribbled on numerous sheets of paper. Jean was a perfectionist and couldn't bear anyone to be involved with her writing when it was in such an unfinished state. David would sort the pages, read them aloud to her, insert a word or alter a comma as she wished, and type them out, but Jean felt she had lost control of her book. She would often be in a rage when either of us was there but she was also unhappy if left alone.

The helpers met for emergency meetings in Sonia's house. Sonia was a good cook and would always make us a splendid lunch. At one of these lunches Sonia said that Jean had told her that she was longing for a holiday. Various destinations were suggested: Paris was no good as Jean would find it too changed, Morocco too far, etc. And then Jo Hill, one of Jean's most devoted helpers, suggested Venice. Jean had never been there; it would hold no memories either good or bad to make her sad.

In February 1977 we arrived at the Danieli and were installed in two adjoining rooms. I didn't know Jo Hill well until this holiday and Jo, being a shy person (and rather a suspicious one), was wary of me. She thought that our twin beds were too close together and after Jean was settled she pushed them as far apart as the space would allow. She considered shifting the oak wardrobe to make a wall between us, but stopped when I started to tease her and promised not to jump on her in the night. Although Jo had been married and had three children, this was followed by a relationship with a woman; perhaps this was why she thought that proximity might provoke uncontrollable lust in me.

But the holiday was wonderful for us all: the sun shone, the shopping was easy, the food delicious and the hotel provided us with a wheelchair to lift Jean up the steps and over the canal bridges. Every evening we sat in the bar, while Jean drank several negronis. Then we would put her to bed at eight o'clock and escape, giggling into the night, to exchange our life histories over dinner.

Devon was still cold and wet when Jean went back there in March; so was Wales and it stayed that way all year. Although my vegetable garden was a flop, with the courgettes put out in early May all dying of frost and the summer beans getting blown over in the July storms, the Tower itself was coming together. With difficulty I started to hang the pictures, but drilling into the stone walls was so hard that it always took me much longer than I had expected and I was often one whisky too many by the time I had finished.

George came down whenever he could and caught his first salmon. Billy came to say goodbye. He was moving out to live with friends.

By the end of September I was feeling rained out and as I'd had an advance for my second book, I booked a ticket to the States and arranged to meet up with John and Jo to go camping in the Appalachian Mountains. My second book was going to be set in Sri Lanka and would be about a spoilt young woman who has a saintly husband and is always running away to exotic places.

When I got back to London there was a major Jean crisis and Sonia wasn't there to help. Sonia had been advised to sell her house and was living in Paris. She had finally discovered the extent of the accountant's duplicity and was using the money from her house sale to bring a court case against him. But, three years later, she died before the case came to court, a case she would certainly have won. Instead, knowing that she was dying, she settled out of court for the copyright which she left to Orwell's son.

Jean loved and trusted Sonia and she missed her. She was now eighty-seven, and she rejected all the solutions to her London winter. An ordinary hotel was out of the question for the staff, and a nursing home, even if disguised as a hotel, was out of the question for Jean.

When we had come back from Venice, Jean stayed with me for a week in London before going back to Devon. I couldn't see any reason why she shouldn't spend the winter with me; and so it was arranged.

I slept on a sofa in George's sitting-room because my bedroom was the most suitable for Jean; it was next door to the bathroom and had double doors that led into a room that she could use as a sitting-room. There was a TV and a record player and we put a small fridge on her bedside table as she often wanted cold milk in the night. It was hard work, but I was good at it: cooking, shopping with her, arranging lunch with friends, finding the right lipstick and trying not to let her drink too much. It was impossible not to love Jean and I wanted to take care of her.

Jean also became quite fond of my mother and the two of them would go off to the pictures together. Sidney Sheldon's *The Other Side of Midnight* was a book she often re-read and when the film came out they saw it through twice.

My affair with Jeremy had started all over again and I felt at the mercy of his moods and infidelities. Jean would comfort me; she knew about heartless men. We would sit on her bed sharing a joint and she would pat my hand and call me 'sweetie'.

George, who had given up his mattress for her (the one on my bed was rather hard), would come up every night and spend the cocktail hour with her. They didn't seem to mind their surreal conversations. George was deaf, Jean's voice was tiny and when Jean told George about the 'Crabtree

Club' he thought they were discussing the fruit tree.

We took Jean to hear George at Ronnie Scott's, to hear him sing the song that she had written.

> It's the sky
> That's never blue
> It's nuts
> Without the chocolate
> It's life
> (*pause*)
> With you.

John Chilton had set it to music and added this middle section to make it a suitable length for a song.

> Through icy seas of silence
> Our salty affair drifts apart
> Feeble detaining gestures
> Won't bring a change of heart.

Up until Christmas things went smoothly, but when I went to the Tower for a long weekend I drove back to find everything had changed. Jean stopped saying that I had 'magics', and, as I could no longer make her happy, I too became miserable and started complaining to anyone who would listen.

Sonia wrote to me from Paris. She knew that Jo Hill had looked after Jean during the weekend when I went to the Tower, but she explained that it didn't prevent Jean from feeling abandoned by me. When things deteriorated further and I became even more desperate, I rang Sonia in Paris for advice. She told me that I must protect myself and that I mustn't stay alone with Jean when I drove her back to Devon.

It was hard for me to acknowledge such failure. Mrs Pefect thought that she would be the one to succeed in making Jean feel secure and happy. I wrote to Sonia, 'I realise I can't do that, I can't even make her feel all right.'

CHAPTER 16

The Ferryman

It was February when I drove Jean back to Devon. The journey was made in an unfriendly silence on her part, and a false chirpiness on mine. Over the last few years her cottage had been made more comfortable and very pretty by Jo Hill. Jo had also been down the previous week to get in some shopping and had arranged the flowers that Sonia had sent from Paris. A woman who lived close by had agreed to become Jean's carer on a daily basis. Thanks to Francis Wyndham, Diana Athill (Jean's editor) and the success of *Wide Sargasso Sea*, Jean's other books were all in print and selling well, so there was now enough money to pay for essential help and proper heating.

I should have been relieved when I left, for Jean and for me, but I drove back feeling guilty and wondering why it had all gone wrong. But it wasn't just pride; I felt a sense of loss, just as I had with Henrietta's children, Caroline and Joshua, after they had gone. If I had ever hoped that I might be better at looking after people and children I wasn't related to, I was wrong.

For the rest of that year I worked on my book about the spoilt wife, and, with the intention of doing bed and breakfasts at the Tower, I was making some improvements to the bedrooms. Peter Eyre had recently spent a weekend with us and I'd asked him if he could think of anything that would make the place more comfortable for visitors. Most people, when asked such a question, would politely reply that everything was perfect. Not Peter. He pointed out that although the incumbents on the first floor had nice cotton sheets, a TV and different views from three windows, they had to go up a floor to a bathroom or downstairs to a shower-room to find a loo. He was right and I drew up plans to carve off a part of the first-floor landing to install a toilet and wash-basin. Encouraged by the success and convenience of this one I asked the builders to put in another for the top-floor bedroom. This attic room had a sloping roof and the toilet had to be squeezed into what had been a clothes cupboard. The builders said that people would bang their heads. Not if they were sitting down, I pointed out. And if they left the door to the bedroom open there was just room to stand in front of the wash-basin. I could now write in my brochure, 'Both bedrooms have en suite toilet and washing facilities.'

In the garden I wanted to plant roses. The vegetables were already taking up all the space at one side of the house, and nearly all of my time. I decided that I would plant climbing roses and they could grow up the fruit trees I'd already planted. By the end of August I had so many different kinds of vegetables that I had to buy a huge chest freezer to store them in. September was spent making vast quantities of sour, insipid plum wine, boiling huge quantities of water to blanch the runner beans for freezing, and chopping onions and tomatoes for chutney. The wine was fermenting in demijohns in front of the cooker and the kitchen throbbed to the sound of the gases escaping through the glass air locks.

Not surprisingly I didn't work hard enough on my book and handed in a manuscript that was full of mistakes. At least the damson jam and tomato chutney turned out well.

In November I decided to get a job, mostly because I wanted to save some money for a winter holiday. The only thing I could think of was to become a minicab driver and so I got out the *Yellow Pages*. Most of the firms just laughed and said they'd never heard of lady minicab drivers, but one, Town and Country, based in Belsize Park, agreed to interview me. I had a clean licence, a four-door Cortina and I could read the *A to Z*.

I was called 'Tango Twelve'. Our controller didn't use our real names when allotting a job and the anonymity of my pseudonym pleased me. Soon I was given all the jobs involving children, old people and any customer who needed their shopping carried in. 'We'll give that one to Tango Twelve,' the controller would say, but he would reward me too, with trips to London Airport and once to Gatwick. One Sunday I was sent to Jonathan and Rachel Miller's house. Susan Sontag was having lunch with them but leaving for New York in the afternoon. We didn't chat on the way to the airport – I was much too nervous, and I had discovered that people like to be quiet when being driven. I was nervous whoever I was driving: I always thought that

I might mis-hear the address, get the time wrong, or lose the way and make someone miss a train. Once I lost Charing Cross station, completely. My very cross female passenger got out near the Embankment, flung a £5 note at me and started running.

All the other drivers had walkie-talkie machines fitted to their cars, but I had decided not to. I thought the crackling reception would make it all the more likely that I wouldn't hear my instructions, so after each job I would go back to the office, park my car and sit inside chatting to the other drivers.

One day I was given an address that I thought was my mother's. She had recently moved and I hadn't been to her new flat. Having retired from her old job as caretaker for a large house of bed-sits in Hampstead, she had been re-housed by the Council. She had told me that her new flat was perfect and that she was allowed to keep her dog. Apart from that brief period when she had lived with us when Tom was born, she had worked in the Hampstead house for twenty-five years.

Once I lived with her in that house. We had one room in the basement; the kitchen was in the passage and we both slept in a small double bed. But as she was recently divorced and probably menopausal, sharing a small space with a lazy teenager was an obvious recipe for trouble. We fought horribly and when I was sixteen I left to get married.

Both of us had been absentee mothers: I had left Patrick with my aunt and hardly saw him for three years and my mother left me boarding in a convent when I was four. It was during the war. She was having an affair with an American serviceman and I was in the way. They used to take me out at the weekend and I had to call him 'Uncle Guy'. I didn't like him because he made a fuss about the white mouse that I always had with me. And my mother herself had also been abandoned. Her mother was a Tiller girl and she left her daughter to be brought up by a family in Southampton. She didn't die until the mid-1960s but my mother never mentioned her and I was almost unaware of her existence. Even in a perfect domestic setting mother and child relations can be hard, and our family's was far from perfect. Mothers are often frightened of their children, and children of their mothers.

These are the excuses I made to myself for my ongoing neglect of my mother. She had now been in her new flat for three months and I hadn't been to see her.

I checked the address I'd been given. 'It's my mother,' I told my controller (who wasn't very interested). 'Where am I taking her?'

'To the hospital,' he replied.

I ran up the steps to the front door and pressed the bell with her name on it. There was an intercom and shortly I heard her voice.

'It's your minicab,' I said.

I heard her coming down the stairs and I stood in the doorway blocking her path. She opened the door, looked at me and went to step round me. I side-stepped too and then she looked at me.

'What are you doing?' she said.

'I'm looking at you,' I replied.

'Why?' She looked down at the front of her blue jersey dress to make sure that the buttons were all done up. She went to step round me again and again I blocked her path.

'What *are* you doing?' she said, rather crossly this time.

'I'm waiting to see if you are going to recognise me.'

She put on her glasses, which were hanging on a string round her neck. She looked at me through them, took them off again and said, 'No, I don't recognise you.'

'Mum, it's Diana.'

'So it is. I thought you said you were the minicab driver.'

'I did. I'm minicabbing, saving up for a holiday.'

She wanted to show me the flat so we went up and had a cup of coffee while I admired everything. Her dog, Simba, and Creamy her large black and white cat were curled up together in a basket. On a chest of drawers were her photographs: my brother looking rather handsome with a Fifties quiff and with a cigarette drooping from his mouth, one of her with me aged about two, and another of me from the days when I was a model. There was one of Candy dressed in her school uniform; it was signed 'to my darling granny'.

George was there, a stage photograph of him all dressed in black and holding a microphone, and one of Tom and Patrick taken at a funfair. The one of Mum and me was in the most prominent position.

'Let's go,' I said. 'You'll be late for your appointment. What's wrong with you anyway?'

'It's this silly cough. If only I could give up the fags. I have cut down, though.'

We pulled up at the out-patients' and she fumbled in her purse for some change. 'Here,' she said and, taking no notice

of my objections, she gave me the money and paid her passage. I drove away with the familiar mixture of relief, guilt and confusion: relief to be free from her physical presence which I found so paralysing, guilt that I had not been able to be loving or friendly, and confusion because I didn't know why I felt like that.

CHAPTER 17

My Last Affair

I had planned the holiday that I was saving up for with my friend Polly Devlin. In 1979, on a cold sunny day in February, we set off from Heathrow and arrived in Freetown, the capital of Sierra Leone, West Africa. There it was hot but cloudy.

We both wanted sun and tans, so this was not an auspicious beginning. Polly was looking very cross as the bus careered through dusty villages to our hotel.

Our room overlooked the sea. 'It's not blue like the Caribbean,' said Polly and stomped off to the bathroom for a shower.

'The water's cold,' she said, emerging two minutes later.

Polly had won a *Vogue* competition for young writers. But she was not only talented and very clever, she was also astonishingly pretty, with blonde hair, a face like a Botticelli angel and a Rubenesque figure. However, when she was cross she looked like a spoilt Pekingese. I had promoted Sierra Leone over Polly's choice of the

Caribbean and therefore it was my job to turn the water from cold to hot.

At the reception desk I was rewarded by huge smiles and promises of hot water to come, and also by a flirtatious look from a guest who closely resembled David Attenborough.

Our hotel was on a long beach and at either end was an outdoor restaurant. We went to the nearest for supper. The food wasn't bad, the clouds had rolled away, the stars came out and millions of white crabs danced on the beach.

Even in those days smokers didn't smoke in the bedroom if sharing with a non-smoker, so I settled down with a book and my roll-up in the lounge.

'How about a readymade?' said David Attenborough's double as he sat down beside me. And so began my last affair.

Lewis was employed by an Anglo-American mining company and was working in Freetown until April. He was rather lonely and more than happy to spend all his evenings and days off with us. Although I behaved like a teenager in love for the first time, Polly remained sympathetic. We lay on our sun beds occasionally cooling off in the sea (which luckily always turned blue by midday), while she listened patiently to me burbling on about what he said and what he could have meant.

I didn't discover that Lewis was a compulsive womaniser until it was too late to avoid getting hurt. Womanisers are obviously good at seduction and Lewis made me feel that none of the women who had gone before me had meant anything. I was the real one – and I fell for it.

By the end of the holiday Lewis had received news of his

next posting. He had been recalled to his head office in Swansea, about an hour's drive from the Tower.

The first time he came to the Tower I sat waiting for him on the wide stone window ledge on the first floor from where I could just get a glimpse of the road. There was no sister to ask, 'Is there anybody coming?' His will be the fifth car. I don't count the lorry. He'll be in the next white car. I went down to the kitchen to get a glass of wine and check the dinner and then I heard his car bumping down the lane.

For the next few months Lewis came to the Tower every night of the week, but at the weekends he went back to his house near Colchester. It seemed ironic that, having come from Essex, I had attempted to reject my past by having a house in Wales and Lewis, coming from the Welsh valleys, had moved there.

His house was at one end of a village and at the other end lived his girlfriend and their daughter Michelle. In Sierra Leone he had simply described himself as 'unmarried'. By the end of the holiday I had become fully aware of the girl-friend; Lewis had sent me out to shop for home-coming presents for her, although he had carefully chosen the ones for his daughter himself.

The life that Lewis led was exhausting. He seldom finished work early and didn't arrive at the Tower until after eight o'clock. He drank a huge amount of vodka every night and always went to bed with a tumbler-full on the table. By the time we got to sleep it was almost six o'clock and time to get up.

At the end of the summer he rented a small semi-detached house on the outskirts of Swansea. Sometimes I went there for the night, shopping for three as Lewis shared it with another engineer called Arthur. I didn't enjoy those evenings. They both watched sport compulsively, and Arthur would line up six cans of lager by his chair and as each one was drunk he would crunch it flat, aim it at the waste bin and miss. In the morning I would pick up the cans, wash up the supper things and head back to the Tower.

Lewis and his friend Arthur were both right-wing conservatives. Lewis's father had been a steelworker and a trade union official. Lewis hardly ever saw his parents but he told me that they kept in close contact with his ex-wife and the son of that early marriage. He had been nineteen and stationed in Ireland when he got the phone call that his girlfriend was pregnant. He came home and married her. Lewis studied for his engineering degree while still in the Army. When his national service came to an end he joined the Anglo-American company he still worked for and his career became so successful that the wife, the baby, the parents and the valleys were soon left far behind.

One incident in Lewis's life had at least saved him from being a racist. After an accident at work where he badly injured his back he came to respect the black doctor who treated him. So although he thought there was no such thing as the deserving poor and hanging was too good for murderers, at least we didn't disagree about apartheid. And if we had? By the time I discovered Lewis's views I was too obsessed to care.

CHAPTER 18

A Sort of Excuse

Two months after my mother's appointment at the hospital she was admitted as an in-patient. When I went to see her she pulled aside her hospital gown and showed me little blue biro marks that had been drawn on her chest. She asked me what they were and I pretended I didn't know. Her question had not been phrased in a way that required an honest answer.

Later that month my brother Alan and I were called in to see the consultant and, standing in the corridor outside my mother's room, he told us that she had a large tumour on her lung, the radiation had failed to shrink it, and the prognosis was not good. Alan was two years older than me, we had been separated first by the war and then again when our parents got divorced. Whenever we tried to become friends, the relationship fizzled out after a few weeks.

Alan and I went to the pub. He called me 'Sis'. I liked that but he referred to my mother as 'Podge'. This affectionate nickname summed up the difference in our attitude to our mother. Alan's was that of a loving son; mine, on the surface, was like Regan's.

It hadn't always been like that. Although we were separated during the war, when it was over I was eight and had gone to live with her in Essex. My father was seldom there and my brother was away at a boarding school. Mum was often unhappy and always depressed. When I came back from school each day she would be lying on her bed, usually crying. I felt it was my job to make her happy and protect her from my father who had an unreliable temper and several girlfriends.

When they were finally divorced, I was fourteen and was sent to live with relatives. It must have been very difficult for my aunt. She was a conventional but kind woman married to a rather bad-tempered doctor. Unlike my mother, she made me go to bed early and I was not allowed to be late for school. I missed the freedom I'd had at home: I was no longer allowed to wear make-up or a padded bra, I couldn't cycle round the village square in the evening giving haughty looks to the boys. I missed my dog, a cocker spaniel called Tuppy.

It was three months before I ran away and joined my mother in her bed-sitting-room, but Tuppy wasn't there; the landlady had insisted that he be got rid of.

Every day I travelled with my mother to work. I was now nearly fifteen and had found a job in a shop round the corner from where she was employed as a cook. In the evening we met at six p.m. at Oxford Circus tube and returned home together. Neither of us had any friends and I felt she was suffocating me. Perhaps, being still relatively young, she felt the same.

Things got easier when our landlady made her the housekeeper. We lived rent-free. Also, there was more money. My first job was in a small shop in Oxford Street, but I saw an advertisement for show girls in my copy of the *Stage*, was interviewed by the owner of the Cabaret Club, lied about my age and got a job as a night-club hostess-cum-show girl. The wages were the same as in the shop but were supplemented by tips from the customers who were also required to buy us cigarettes and a spray of flowers.

The club closed at two o'clock and I would slide into bed beside my mother leaving the money and the boxes of Black Russian Sobranie on the mantelpiece. In the morning she would quietly leave the room, clean the rest of the house and then bring in my breakfast on a tray around midday. This arrangement continued until I got married.

Our inappropriate dependence and closeness damaged our relationship. Apart from the time she had come to live with me and George when Tom was born, and I was a needy child again, I kept her at arm's length.

After her radiotherapy, she left hospital and went to live with Alan and his family in Essex. She still didn't seem to know what was wrong with her and sometimes would phone me and say, 'Di darling, what's this awful pain I've got in my side?'

But I didn't let her pain or her words touch me. She was re-admitted to hospital the week before she died. It was a dismal dingy place. I walked into a large, old-fashioned ward with windows so high up that very little light came through. The beds, about twenty of them, were so close together that you could sit on one and talk to the person in the next bed without straining your back.

Nobody had told me where my mother was and I walked slowly down the centre aisle looking for her. She looked very tiny, the huge swelling on her chest making her body, which had shrunk as the cancer progressed, seem even smaller. The pain clouded her eyes and for the second time in her life she didn't recognise me. I didn't stay long. I caught the train to Liverpool Street, crossed over to Paddington and went back to Wales and Lewis's grim little semi near Swansea. He looked at me and I realised perhaps for the first time how important my appearance was to him. 'No gloomy faces here,' he said, and I went to the kitchen to make supper.

CHAPTER 19

Marriage Flowers and Funeral Meats

George's visits to the Tower often coincided with Lewis's. They had little in common, but would sometimes go off to the pub together. At first George had been anxious that Lewis, unlike my previous hippy lovers, might seduce me away permanently. When it became obvious that this was not the case, they settled down into a blokey relationship over darts and whisky. George couldn't drive and was pleased to have someone with a car who would take him to the pub as his moped was often out of petrol.

Sometimes my friends met Lewis too and on the whole were mystified by my infatuation. Penelope Tree thought he must be a spy. Anne Wollheim always referred to him as 'that very peculiar boyfriend', another said, 'Isn't he a bit middle management for you?' And Polly, when writing about our African holiday for a Sunday paper, said that I wouldn't have looked twice at him across a London drawing-room.

Lewis went away for August with his family on a camping holiday. He borrowed my sleeping bags and I felt pleased that something of mine had gone with him.

While he was away I tried to pull the garden back into shape. My mother was not the only thing that had been neglected. Lettuces went to seed, pea-pods shrivelled and turned yellow, the runner beans were stringy, the currant bushes weren't netted and so the birds had a feast.

But the garden work came to an abrupt end when, a week after my mother's funeral, Alan rang me to say that my father had lung cancer. He was still living with Marion, the woman for whom he had left my mother twenty-five years ago. I had never forgiven him. He had occasionally visited us in NW1 and although George would always give him a drink I never asked him to stay for a meal.

When I was married to my first husband, Patrick's father, I had sometimes been so broke that I would go to my father for money. He was working as a clerk for British Rail at the time and I would sit on his desk, swing my legs and ask him for a pound. He would look round proudly at his fellow workers and feel in his back pocket for the money.

My father had often embarrassed me: when I was a young teenager he had seemed too aware of my sexuality, he made jokes that I only half understood and once took me to see a Phyllis Dixie show. This piece of theatre consisted of young women posed on the stage as Greek statues. Pieces of chiffon were draped around their hips, but their breasts were bare. They didn't move, not even the blink of an eye, and if they had the Lord Chamberlain would have closed the show.

As soon as my father became ill he turned into a person I

wished I had bothered to know. The first thing he did was to marry Marion, something she had always wanted.

When Alan rang, George was away performing in Edinburgh and Patrick was on holiday with Kate, so only Tom and Candy came with me to his wedding reception. I always remembered Marion as a vivacious young woman with scarlet nails wearing a black and white swagger coat. Here she was, middle-aged and with greying hair; and, no longer a skinny school-girl, I was now the glamorous one in a black dress with a slit up the side, ankle strap shoes and a brightly coloured jacket.

There is a photograph of the wedding party. Helen, my brother's second wife, is there, looking a little anxious, but perhaps she knows that she is soon to be replaced by wife No. 3. Standing next to me are Alan and Tom, both of them now nearly the same height as my father. He used to be 6 foot 2, but like my mother he too had shrunk. His mouth and jaw were clenched throughout the short ceremony because he was trying not to cough.

Back at their house in Finchley, off the North Circular Road, we drank lots of white wine and ate sausage rolls. When they were all in the garden, I looked at his books to see if there was anything there that would be able to remind me of him. I stole a semi-pornographic book by an American writer. Once my father had left it in my bedroom and made me promise not to read it.

When they trooped back inside my father was making jokes. He said he didn't think his marriage would last long; he hoped the wedding flowers would last for the funeral.

A week later he was back in hospital. Alan went to see him and said that Dad had minded that he could no longer find his penis. 'It's like searching for a little wren in the hedge,' he told Alan.

Three days he was in the hospital and then he rang me in Wales. 'This is goodbye. I told the doctor that I've had enough, my family has had enough and the staff here have probably had enough. They're going to give me an extra shot tonight.'

I walked down to the river and sat on the bank.

CHAPTER 20

The Seagull and Creamy

When my mother died I inherited Creamy her cat, a creature I came to loathe. Creamy was like the ghost of my mother: she seemed to resemble her, but perhaps only in the guilt I felt at not being able to love her, or to have loved my mother.

My father's ghost appeared very briefly. When I was sitting on the bank of the river at about the time of his death, a lone seagull began to circle and swoop lower and lower over my slumped body. I got up and walked along the bank and the seagull appeared to be following me. I was feeling so emotional about losing the only father I'd ever had, and had never known for long enough to love, that I became convinced it had come back to watch over me.

Once, when I was about twelve, I was picked up by a soldier from our nearby garrison town, and saw my father following us along the beach. When my soldier and I lay down between the beach huts, I knew my father was nearby. I pushed the soldier off me, shook off the sand and ran home. My father was sitting in the kitchen when I got back and did not make any comment. I felt angry and spied-upon, and not until much later did I realise that his motives were not prurient, but probably showed concern for my safety.

The seagull just hung around for half an hour. Creamy was there to stay.

We had recently moved to a house off the north end of the Portobello Road. It was cheap because the area had not yet become fashionable; also because the house was a mess. All the rooms had been divided into boarding-house bedrooms with a leaky wash-basin in each one and the basement, with a separate entrance from the main house, was damp and dark. This would eventually become the kitchen with my bedroom and bathroom leading off it. George's sitting-room took up the ground floor, with bedrooms for Tom, Candy and George on the two floors above.

But that was all in the future, and meanwhile we squashed into the little half-rooms and I cooked in a cubby-hole off the narrow hall. Luckily, Tom was still away at school and Candy at college. Unluckily, the Tower was lent to friends for the winter. This was mostly because of the cats Desmond and Sheba: they had started refusing to travel back to London, and even before I knew I was leaving they sensed it and would disappear. My friends would look after the Tower and the garden, leaving me free to divide my time between the builders in London and Lewis in Wales.

George was very happy. He had a new girlfriend, a young art student who was very keen on him, and also a commission for a new book about his childhood.

For me it was a horrible time. In Swansea Lewis talked constantly about his next posting which he hoped would be anywhere except Wales. He also hoped he could take his daughter and her mother.

In London, Creamy was always waiting for me and relieved that Desmond and Sheba were left behind in Wales. Creamy was a large, fat black-and-white cat with a very pink nose. Her nature was alternately bullying and cringing. In my small half room there was no room for a bedside table so I used the mantelpiece above the bed for my things. Every morning at five o'clock Creamy would knock things off it onto my face: books, pots of face cream, alarm clock and glasses of water. When shouted at, she would jump on top of the stack of cardboard boxes that held my clothes and manage to stare at me in a way that seemed both malevolent and pitiful. Sometimes she would jump on top of me, but the last straw was when she took to shitting in the bath. Perhaps if I had been there all the time, and not always running off to an increasingly uncaring Lewis, we might have bonded and, loved as my mother had loved her, she would have been persuaded to use her litter tray. But as half the week I was sitting in Lewis's unfriendly little house, Creamy continued to use the bath and our cleaner said she would have to leave. As usual, I turned to George. He took Creamy to the vet and she was put down.

CHAPTER 21

Patrick

My affair with Lewis and my parents' death meant that I could avoid confronting Patrick's heroin addiction. If there was a moment when he told me, or a moment when I didn't know, followed by a moment when I did, I don't remember it. Did he ever say, 'Mum, I've got something to tell you'? Did George and I say to each other, 'Do you think Patrick . . .'? Did Kate confide in me? Did a friend tell me? Did common sense inform me of the obvious? I don't remember. When did he cross the danger line? I don't know. I don't remember.

That winter we tried to help him and his life was improving: he and his girlfriend Kate were happy together, his electrical business was doing well and his GP was maintaining him on methadone.

Then he relapsed. I bailed him out for the last time from a police station in Dover. It was New Year's Day and I had been at Ronnie Scott's seeing the New Year in with George when I got the familiar phone call. I went home, bathed and changed and set off when it was still dark. Patrick was chatting in a friendly way with the desk sergeant when I arrived; they both knew the form. I signed the bail papers and we drove back to London.

The sun was up, it was cold, but the sky was a brilliant blue and the trees, draped with old man's beard, were sparkling with frost. He told me that the incident, speed and smack, was just a hiccup. I didn't really believe him and, thinking that it would improve his prospects when his case came to court, I asked Justin, the psychiatrist friend from Release, to help. He referred Patrick to the drug rehabilitation centre at the Middlesex Hospital and we were taken on as a family. There was a disastrous omission to this plan. It was 1980 and partners were not treated as they are now. Kate, who had loved and cared for him, was not offered the counselling that was available for George and me. She felt isolated and rejected, and she decided to go to Egypt to study for her degree in Arabic and Russian.

Our sessions at the Middlesex did not last long. We could only be seen if we all turned up and, more often than not, one of us made an excuse.

One morning when I was sitting in Lewis's home trying to write a short story, the phone started ringing. Unless it rang in a certain way I wasn't allowed to answer it in case it was Lewis's girlfriend. This time it rang twice, stopped, and then rang again. I picked it up and George told me that Patrick was getting married that week, not to Kate who had now been gone for two months, but to an eighteen-year-old girl from Brazil. George had been asked to the wedding but I had not. I knew that I could have gone but I didn't want to.

I loved Kate and thought that Patrick still did too. He had never mentioned Paula, the new girl, and if it was just an arrangement to give her a green card I felt there was no reason for me to be there.

It was Friday, Lewis drove me up to London and I had supper with George who had just been to the wedding. He said that Paula was really sweet, but seemed very young.

The following day I worked hard in the house. The builders had finished but there were still all the boxes to unpack. That evening I went over to Anne Wollheim's to play bridge. Knowing I would be drinking, Anne had suggested that I could sleep there. Long after I'd gone to bed George came round and he and Anne sat up drinking whisky and tea. At eight o'clock he opened my bedroom door and standing half in and half out of the room said, 'Patrick's dead.'

I don't know what happened next. At some moment Tom appeared. George and Anne had rung his school, and then rung Candy. George disappeared. He had been asked to identify the body. I just lay on the sofa.

Some years before this a friend from Wales had rung me in London. She said she was speaking from a call box at a nearby tube station and that someone had been run over and killed. The phone line was crackling and I hadn't heard the name of the victim. I don't know why, I assumed it was an animal and not a family member. But when I went to fetch her, it transpired that it was Toby, her son. 'I didn't know what else to do with myself,' she said. And that was how I felt.

George was dealing with the police and all the formalities, it was too early for the condolence letters, and apart from Kate I didn't know any of his friends that I could or should ring. It's quite different when an older person dies: there's a life that has to be sorted out, wills to be found and read, belongings and clothes to be sent to charities, perhaps pets to be found a home for, children and grandchildren to be contacted. Patrick was not quite twenty-five, and like my friend, Toby's mother, I didn't know what to do or how to fill the emptiness. And it was emptiness; pain came later.

The next day, Sunday, Anne made us all supper and then somebody remembered Paula. George had picked up Patrick's address book and diary from the police station. I found her number and dialled it. 'Where is he, where is he?' she was saying, and I told her, just like that, 'He's dead.' I gave her Anne's address and she came round in a taxi.

After the wedding she had given Patrick £100 and he had gone back to his room to collect his things. They had arranged to meet again that evening in her flat off Baker Street. When he didn't come back, she hadn't known what to do and had spent the weekend imagining the worst. But usually the worst doesn't happen.

The worst was that Patrick, who had not used heroin for several weeks, had bought some with her £100 and also a half bottle of whisky. He packed up his room, perhaps thought about what he was doing, put his photos of Kate in a box, found an old syringe and then drank most of the whisky. The whisky made him vomit, but by that time the quantity of heroin, which he could no longer tolerate, made him pass out and, unable to clear his throat and lungs, still unconscious, he choked to death.

CHAPTER 22

The Funeral

Patrick's death was in the newspaper: it was a front-page story in the *Daily Mail*. Under the heading 'Jazz man's son dies of heroin' was a photograph of me wearing a miniskirt and leaning my head on George's shoulder.

I didn't lean on him now. Instead I shot off down to Swansea, Lewis and sex. Perhaps I expected more sympathy from him than I had received after my parents died. I didn't get it. At least I'd had more sense than to drive there, but on the train I had a few vodkas. Lewis looked at me with some distaste and just said, 'No tears, end of story.' And he and Arthur went off to the pub.

When he came back we went up to bed and he brought some of Arthur's sex magazines upstairs with him. 'Choose the girl you most fancy,' he said, 'and tell me what you'd like me to do to you both.'

I stayed at the house for three days. Without the car I couldn't go anywhere, but I was still numb and anyway there was nowhere to go, except home, where I should have gone.

For the first time in my life I started to masturbate. Every morning, after I'd picked up the crumpled beer cans and done the washing up, I crept up the stairs, closed the flimsy curtains and climbed between the nylon sheets. In the afternoon I did the same.

But I dreaded the nightly sessions with the magazines. In one of them were photographs of Jessica, who had been Patrick's girlfriend before Kate. They had met in Paris when Patrick was with the Magic Circus. Much later Jessica had told me that she had only become a model to help Patrick when his heroin debts had become dangerous. In the magazine Jessica was shown in a series of photos demonstrating fellatio. The first picture showed her leaning over a wash-basin with her bum pointing provocatively towards the camera. She was cleaning her teeth; the story-line was about the importance of cleanliness and sex. As I hadn't seen Patrick naked since he was a baby, I had no idea if the male in the pictures was him or not.

At the end of the week Lewis drove me back to London. He was going home to Essex so he dropped me off at the North Circular and I got the tube to Ladbroke Grove. No one was in the house when I got back. George was away on tour, Candy was doing an art course and staying with friends near her college, and Tom was back at school. He was playing Oberon in *The Dream* and it was the dress rehearsal that weekend, otherwise he would have been allowed to come home.

I poured some vodka into a mug and picked up a large pile of condolence letters. One was just signed 'M' and for a minute I couldn't think who that was, and then I recognised handwriting I hadn't seen for twenty-four years. It was Michael's, Patrick's father: he was offering to help with the coroner or the funeral. The head master of Patrick's comprehensive wrote of his charm and good humour, others described him as 'bright and original', 'kind, attractive and generous', 'adorable, well mannered and courteous' and Maudie, George's eighty-six-year-old mother, wrote 'he had such a large heart'.

The funeral took place at Golders Green crematorium. Justin, the psychiatrist who had got Patrick on to the Middlesex rehab programme, spoke about Patrick's battle with his addiction. He also spoke about Patrick's sad daily life and how he had been left by me with an aunt when he was only two years old. He tried to exonerate me from blame, stressing that I had been only seventeen when Patrick was born. Tom read 'Dust' by Rupert Brooke, Simon Cutter, an actor friend of Patrick, read 'Fear no more the heat of the sun'. I wanted 'The Pulley' by George Herbert, but I can't remember if anybody read it.

We all trooped out into a freezing March day while a Jimi Hendrix track played. As it ended, a taxi drew up and out sprang a tall bearded man in a fur-collared coat who put his arms round me and apologised for being late. Not until we were back at Rachel and Jonathan Miller's house for the wake did I realise that the man who had missed the funeral was Michael, the absentee father.

I had sobered up during the service and was beginning to remember that I had been too drunk to go to the undertaker's that morning to look at Patrick's body. I've finally forgiven myself many things connected with Patrick's life and death, but I still wish that I'd done that. And I should have remembered the importance of it. When I was working at Release I accompanied Bob, a fellow worker, back to his mother's house in an old-fashioned part of the East End. His mother had just died and all his aunts and siblings were waiting for him to go in and pay his last respects. He was so frightened that I went in ahead of him. I leant forward and kissed the woman on the forehead, it seemed such an easy, natural thing to do, and then Bob did the same.

CHAPTER 23

The Aftermath

The following week I drove back to the Tower. Delith and Roy, my friends who had looked after the house and the cats all winter, had now managed to find a place of their own nearby. Delith asked if she could take Desmond and Sheba with her when they left and Roy said he would continue to take care of the garden.

Lewis had gone away for several weeks, he wouldn't say where, and in spite of advice from George and many others I often stayed alone at the Tower. At weekends friends were able to come, George had a long fishing break and during the Easter holidays Tom and Candy were there. Tom had a poem published in his school magazine.

Brother Ashes

'My brother's dead'
The few that heard quickly turned away.
'My brother's dead'

They gave up listening, hearing, seeing, feeling
(as if they ever did).
They'd never met him, known him, loved him or cried
    for him
When there was nothing else to do.
It made no difference in their little worlds
Whether he breathed air
Or they breathed him.
Do they actually forget at times,
Even when I'm there?
Why not?
They never knew he existed
Until he didn't.
Will I run too and change the subject,
Turn away and cross the street, deaf to death,
When the other voices call,
'My brother's dead,'
Or will I turn to them and say
'My cry has echoed too through empty ears'
Will I hold them and cry for theirs or mine or all,
Or no brothers?
Time has etched his memory deeper.
Too solid now to break.
Yet I no longer cry for him,
Have I squeezed him dry?
Did the poppy of that etching smart at first
And then disappear?
And you few who heard,
Why did you warm and comfort me,
When it was my brother who needed warmth.

My wounds have healed,
Yet my brother is still dead,
And others are still dying.

Candy, who had been closest to Patrick, felt isolated but I was too self-absorbed to comfort her. No one could comfort me either. George was desperate that he was unable to, but I felt frozen with grief and guilt. Tom rang nearly every night. The first time, for a moment, I thought it was Patrick.

The Telephone

The good one rang on time tonight
And left me choked with tears.
It sounded like the bad one's voice,
The one that used to call.

Will it be the police this time?
Has there been a raid?
The good one rings to say hello,
The bad one to accuse.

I used to dread the bad one's calls
The pleas and endless lies.
Why are their voices so alike?
The words are not the same.

Is it yet another crash?
Do you just want bail?
The good one rings to say hello,
The bad one to complain.

Too late to say I'll listen now
The good one's on the line.
Too late to say I'll try again
The good one's full of news.

Have you lost your job again?
Do you want some cash?
The good one rings to say hello
The bad one just to moan.

The bad one didn't ring that night
Instead it was the morgue.
The good one rings to comfort me
The bad one, not at all.

In the attic I had a box of the children's papers: school reports, drawings and letters they had written to me. An old exercise book of Patrick's contained the punishment essays we had set him for minor misdemeanours. One began 'I must not make sick noises when I don't like my food', another started 'I must not always correct Mummy in front of other people'. There were his scrapbooks: the Kennedy assassination, the first moon landing and some photographs of Bertrand Russell. When Patrick was five I took him to hear Russell speak against the bomb in Trafalgar Square and the photograph was a memento of that occasion.

I spent the days sitting at the kitchen table at the Tower shuffling the papers, re-reading the condolence letters and answering them. So many people said that there was no need to reply, but what else was there to do all day? At night I dreamed that he floated outside my window; he was always beckoning me. During the day I tried to write a poem about it.

Spring

On sunny days like this I miss you most.
Perhaps not miss, just wish that you could see them too.
But as you were, not as this tiring ghost.
Green fields, alive and beautiful, sky blue,
The sun that burns on me and can't reach you.
It's hard to see the point of all the pain,
Surrounded by this showy force of life.
Could I forget and rest in grey and rain,
And stop the fight to try to keep you near,
While you return to fester in these awful dreams?
Not dead: moving, smiling, beckoning me there.
I will not go. Not yet. For I can see
That sad and lonely side which I passed on to you,
The side that kills is only half of me.

Sometimes, thinking that I would feel better in London, I would gather up the letters and drive up the M4. Patrick's wife had gone home to her parents, but before she left she had brought round an old suitcase with his things. There wasn't much: a cigarette lighter, an invoice book, a poster of Che Guevara and some old T-shirts; no books or records and I assumed he'd sold all those.

One afternoon when I was sitting with the case trying to decide what to throw away and what to keep, Venetia rang for George and I answered the phone. It was about two o'clock, she must have realised that I had been drinking and she suggested coming round with some lunch. When she arrived I was sitting on the floor and crying. George came in and went straight to his desk to deal with his messages, and Venetia said, 'I don't know if you've noticed, but your wife is having a nervous breakdown.'

By the following afternoon Justin had got me admitted to the Bethlem Hospital, the world's oldest psychiatric hospital, once known as Bedlam. On arrival a list of my belongings was recorded and I signed it: shorts, jeans, T-shirts, comb, family allowance book and photographs, etc. The nurse who showed me to my little room was gentle, but the one who forced pills down me when I woke screaming in the night was less so. A beautiful garden surrounded the building and sometimes Justin would come and take me for a gloomy walk through the shrubbery. Every morning and evening we had group therapy sessions run by Dr Geraldine, who attempted to stop me trying to run the group. I made friends with Betty, a young girl who was manic depressive. She explained that being manic was horrible, all right on the way up, but once there, completely exhausting. She didn't mind being depressed as she could just lie in a ball on her bed; it was only bad when she got suicidal.

After two weeks I was considered well enough to go home. Anne Wollheim drove George down to fetch me. I said tearful goodbyes to Betty and to Geraldine; there are few secrets between patients in psychiatric wards and friendships are intense and important. Betty and I wrote to each other for over a year, but we never met again.

CHAPTER 24

Writer in Residence

S oon after leaving the hospital I was back in Wales, making summer puddings, strawberry jam and doing battle with the birds who as usual were trying to eat all the fruit from my currant bushes. Then, in June, Bruce Chatwin came to stay.

The previous autumn he had walked over from his publisher's cottage to have supper with me and a mutual friend who was staying at the Tower. I had met him before, but I found his blond good looks and the stream of often unintelligible chatter quite intimidating. I was both impressed by and shy of him. On that early visit Bruce spotted that I could cook, and that the top room, with only a small window and rather cut off from the rest of the house, would be ideal for writing. Early the following year he wrote to me from America tentatively inviting himself to stay; he enticingly suggested that we could take it in turns to make supper as then we could both write.

Bruce stayed with me off and on for five years and never even made a cup of tea, although he did occasionally boil up some rather disgusting-smelling Mexican leaves into a brew which he said gave him energy – not something I thought he lacked, rather he fizzed with it. But if Bruce, with his endless demands for coffee, company, meals and an ear for his latest pages, did nothing to enable me to write, he did get me out of the house. We went to Pembrokeshire and climbed around on the Preselis, the mysterious hills where the stones for Stonehenge were quarried. We climbed a few mountains, Bruce talking all the time as he strode ahead. Unlike me he didn't smoke, so, in spite of the stream of anecdotes, he always had more puff than I did.

When Bruce, friends, or any of the family stayed with me in Wales I was so busy with cooking and gardening that I could cope with my depression. But when I was on my own I quickly began to despair.

It didn't seem any better in London, and, partly because of my vegetable garden, and always hoping that Lewis might appear, I wanted to stay in Wales. Since my last visit after Patrick's death, Lewis had discouraged me from going to Swansea and, remembering how bleak I had felt there, I didn't really mind. My face looked more ravaged than it had when I was in Sierra Leone; people were no longer surprised when they learnt my age – forty-four. The burka is a terrible way that men can tyrannise women about their appearance, but it's not the only way.

When Lewis did come to the Tower, he seemed to prefer it if there were other people there too. I refused to acknowledge how much he was abusing me and my hospitality. He didn't even bring his own vodka any more, but I really knew that my misery bored him.

Almost the only enjoyable time we spent together that year was when Bruce got us all in to a France–Wales rugby match. Lewis was enormously impressed by Bruce getting the tickets, as they were changing hands for huge sums of money. And Bruce didn't seem to find Lewis all that odd. Although he liked famous people and titles, he was not at all snobbish; nearly everyone interested him. He was also thoughtful in unexpected ways: he didn't know Candy well but when her Italian boyfriend was killed in a car accident, he wrote a sympathetic letter to her.

In November Bruce left for the winter, Lewis was posted to France and, once the last apple was picked, the potatoes stored, the onions strung up and the autumn broad beans sown, I moved back to London.

Staying at the Tower from the spring to the autumn had become a pattern, it wasn't completely selfish or arbitrary. George loved it there and came during those months as often as he could to write and fish, but the Tower was not a domestic environment that he could manage on his own. In London there was always someone around to change a light bulb for him and show him that the kettle must also be switched on at the wall.

At the Tower, if I wasn't in residence, he might well stumble around in the dark and the cold and go hungry. Who else would chop the wood, make the soup, and encourage the Rayburn to produce some heat and hot water? Sometimes his beloved moped would (mysteriously to him) run out of petrol and down by the river he'd lose his hearing aid, his torch and his glasses. It would have been difficult to ask a girlfriend down; he went fishing until after dark, and what would they have done in an environment which was so markedly mine? London was different. We had our own bedrooms. The sitting-room was in George's taste – Surrealist, and armchairs covered in pale pink silk. My room was next to the kitchen, an area that was definitely my territory. Since we left NW1, eight years ago, we hadn't slept together. Up until Patrick's death, in spite of the affairs and increasingly separate lives, we remained close: I often went to hear him sing, I proof-read his books and articles and I cared about his comfort. We gave each other a kind of stability, and the lack of physical passion ruled out any jealousy on my part and made it possible for George to enjoy guilt-free promiscuity. Patrick's death changed our relationship. I became cold, stiff and unbending. George tried with hugs, squeezed hands and many expressions of love to console me. I became even colder, and it began to seem inevitable that we would separate.

My friendship with Bruce helped me. He realised that although I didn't want to be on my own, I wanted to be left alone. We felt affection towards each other, but it was an affection based on friendship and we were easy in each other's company.

After Christmas Bruce wrote and asked me if he could come back when the weather warmed up and finish writing his book *On the Black Hill*. He asked if Francis Wyndham could also be invited to stay. Jean Rhys was not the only writer whom Francis had helped and encouraged: there were many others who found his understanding of their work invaluable; Bruce was one of them. It was a propitious request. Francis had finally decided to collect and publish Jean's letters and he asked me to co-edit them. It followed that we would be spending a lot of time together and this could just as easily be at the Tower as in London. Francis was Jean's literary executor, she had trusted him and because she hoped that no one would write her biography, Francis decided that the letters might satisfy the curiosity that people felt about Jean. Ultimately her biography was written by Carole Angier. Francis was unable in the end to resist such a sympathetic admirer of Jean's work and he realised that not only would it prevent more unscrupulous biographers attempting to unravel Jean's unhappy life, but it would also keep her books read and in print.

One other thing happened over the winter that helped to salvage our marriage. After Christmas I went into therapy at the Tavistock.

CHAPTER 25

The Tavi

The Tavistock in Hampstead is a psychoanalytic clinic with several aims and programmes. It not only tries to help people, including children and adolescents, with their various depressions, but it is also a teaching institution for would-be analysts. One of their programmes in 1982 was a bereavement study, and I was offered counselling if I would permit the sessions to be videoed.

Every Thursday I drove from the Tower to Newport station and caught the train to London. One morning my car wouldn't start. I yelled up the stairs to Bruce, who came clattering down (he was very flat-footed), jumped on his bike and cycled down the lanes to my friend Anthea. Bruce was always good in an emergency, less wonderful with everyday domestic life.

Anthea heard him charging up the stairs to her bedroom where she was lying naked in bed.

'Quick,' he said, 'Di needs help. You must drive her to Newport or she'll miss the train.'

Anthea reported that he stood watching her as she pulled on her knickers and dress, not in a lascivious way, just curious.

I doubt that my sessions at the Tavi were much use to anyone except me. My analyst was called Dr Hildebrand, a tall, serious-looking man in his late forties, and he allowed me the privilege of having the video camera turned off if I couldn't bear certain things to be recorded. I always asked for it to be switched off if I was talking about sex, and in particular masturbation. There would also be long pauses when the only sound would be of me weeping into the Kleenex which were kept in a handy box on the table, and Dr Hildebrand sighing, perhaps at the bleak stories of my neglect of Patrick.

The other problem was the video camera, or rather Dr Hildebrand's inability to operate it. He may have read Freud, Klein and others, but the instruction book for the video was beyond him. He would spend the first ten minutes struggling with it. Sometimes it would work, but more often not, so our sessions would proceed unrecorded.

Francis Wyndham and I now had a contract from André Deutsch to edit Jean's letters and so he often came down to the Tower for us to work on them. In fact it was only because of Francis's generosity that I was called a co-editor, as he wrote all the notes and had known and befriended Jean for so long. But he liked – we both liked – reading and discussing the letters. Also the excitement of finding a new batch and sitting by the pond to read them over a drink was something better shared.

The presence of Francis at the Tower was also proving

important to Bruce who would read aloud his day's work to him every evening. It was becoming an easier year: George, Francis and Bruce all liked each other, I was busy cooking for them and George was bringing home the trout. And then George got a letter from Pandora.

Since George's first wife had left him, stating clearly that Pandora, though born when she was still married to George, was Tim Whidborne's child, we had heard nothing of them. Tim had written to George at the time saying that he accepted her as his daughter and that he would pay for her education and make provision for her in his will.

Now, twenty years later, Pandora wrote to George saying that she knew that *he* was her father. George wrote back explaining that he was only her father legally and that he wasn't her biological one. It was true that there had been one occasion when he could have fathered her, but Tim and Victoria had been in love at the time and were having an affair. Also, Victoria had said the baby was Tim's.

Pandora's letter was disturbing, but we hoped that George's letter would resolve things. Then, the next month, Pandora turned up at a jazz club where George was playing in Devon, near where she lived with her mother. George was stunned – she looked like him and like our son Tom. Suddenly Pandora's paternity was no longer in doubt.

All the family, except me, were thrilled, and of course Pandora was. Tom had fantasies that he would have an innocent but incestuous love affair with his new sister. Candy had a few reservations and said, 'Now I'm not only not the *real* daughter, I'm not even the *only* one', but she was not greatly affected by it. Her own father, Johnnie, had married twice after his divorce from me, and she had so many steps, and halves, that one more made little difference. Also, unlike Tom, she wasn't living at home. She had spent three months in New York working in a delicatessen and then a year in Paris as an au pair. She often came back for a night or two, but not to live.

I was the odd one out. I felt the hole in my family that had been created by Patrick's death was being filled by someone who was nothing to do with me. Jealousy, fear and panic arose and a feeling that there was now this other family of George, Tom, Pandora and Victoria, from which I was excluded. I was an outsider with no place, no role and no control.

The day came when she was coming to our house for the first time, to stay for a weekend. I made up a bed for her and went out to have a facial. She was in the sitting-room when I got back, probably as nervous as I was.

That evening I made a roast chicken dinner and invited Francis as my support. Pandora told us that her mother was known as 'Beauty' and I was glad I'd had the facial. As soon as the last spoonful of ice cream was downed, Tom got up to go to bed; being deaf in one ear and addicted to his sleep, he never lingered long at the table. One by one he kissed us goodnight and when he'd kissed Pandora she said, 'And don't forget to kiss your other little sister.' Her remark annoyed me. I made no allowances for her tactlessly expressed, but enormous desire, to become part of our family. Tom wouldn't forget to kiss Candy, and anyway both she and Pandora were *big* sisters by two or three years.

I knew that it was going to be difficult for me to make her

feel welcome, and as the house mother I knew that it was up to me. But the timing was bad: once there had been three children, then only two, now there were three again. I knew I couldn't do it. Whenever she came to stay (and at first it was about once a month), I was polite, I gave her clean sheets and showed her how the central heating worked, but I never sat down and talked to her. I had made Caroline and Josh feel they belonged in our family; I couldn't do the same for Pandora. Perhaps she didn't want me to, but her early life and the confusion as to her paternity gave her every reason to need more from us. In the end we all let her down: Tom fell out of love quite quickly, and although George gave her an allowance and paid for some therapy, he didn't give her much fatherly love.

As if her physical resemblance to her half brother Tom was not enough, her similarity in character to George made further proof of her identity unnecessary. She could write and she could sing. One night, when George was appearing at Ronnie Scott's and was down in the bar entertaining his

fans, Pandora got up on the stage, announced herself and sang two numbers, 'My Heart Belongs to Daddy' and 'Moon River'. George forgot that his career began in a similar way, when he pushed his way to the front of the stage and tricked Humphrey Lyttleton into letting him sing; and Pandora's bold attempt to seduce his audience infuriated him. Even a daughter can seem like a rival, and after a few years they more or less stopped seeing each other.

CHAPTER 26

Writer in Residence No. 2

Although Bruce had finished writing *On the Black Hill* he still came to stay at the Tower. That year, 1982, another writer arrived, Molly Parkin. She and her husband, the painter Patrick Hughes, had been friends of ours since the 1960s. Molly came from the Welsh Valleys, but her talents had taken her first to art school in London and eventually to the *Sunday Times* where she had been an inspired, if eccentric, fashion editor. She was dark and almost beautiful, with a cuddly soft shape and an aura of talcum powder and menthol cigarettes. She loved men and sex and she loved to shock.

Molly had written several mildly pornographic books and that year, recently separated from Patrick Hughes, she was somewhat on her uppers and anxious to finish another one. I invited her to stay for as long as she needed to, rather pleased that I couldn't be accused of intellectual snobbery with regard to my resident writer.

She didn't help in the house any more than Bruce did, but

she was good at weeding, and her humour and sympathetic manner made the hours spent in the garden a time when I felt I could tell her anything. She never disapproved and she was a good listener.

Eventually the regime of writing, weeding and listening to me whingeing began to pall for her. Her ex-husband had sent her a huge black dildo and clearly this was not adequate for Molly's needs. I was also beginning to irritate her. When I asked her to put the dildo in a drawer before Yvette, our cleaner, arrived, she would deliberately leave it on her pillow and accuse me of being prudish. So when she started borrowing the car and driving over to her old home in the Valleys, I was relieved, and knew she would soon find a man.

Bruce came down for a long weekend in June and, finding me with a bad back and rather distraught over Molly's increasingly erratic behaviour, said he was taking me to Patmos to stay with his friend, the painter Teddy Millington-Drake. Bruce had decided that my back problem was connected with trouble in the home. He was not above alternative explanations for muscular ailments. I thought no digging or weeding for a fortnight might help too.

Teddy had been dreading our arrival. He loved Bruce, but found him very demanding and he thought that I would harangue him with left-wing, feminist views. I wasn't longing to meet him either. I knew that he was rich, some people thought spoilt, and that he was a friend of Venetia's. He had intended to settle us in and then go to Italy, where he had another house. Unexpectedly, we got on, and he stayed. We had nothing much in common and he said I had the dirtiest fingernails he'd ever seen, but there was one thing which established a close friendship: Teddy still mourned the death of his sister, and I mourned Patrick.

One evening, while lounging in the garden under the plumbago and sipping a cocktail, I was called to the phone.

'Now listen, girl,' said Molly, 'get yourself a drink, the news is bad.'

'Who's dead?' I asked.

'Listen,' she went on, 'you've got your good friends with you. Are you sitting down?'

'Molly, please tell me.'

At last she said, 'You've been busted.'

I laughed, said goodbye, and hung up.

As well as the forty-two different vegetables I grew, there were also my cannabis plants. I had built a makeshift greenhouse out of polythene sheets to give them ideal conditions and they had flourished. There were ten of them and some were nearly six feet high. In amongst them were the tomato plants, not doing quite so well owing to the excessive amount of shade that the cannabis plants provided. Molly never smoked dope, drink was her drug, but she had promised to water the plants.

I knew that since my parents and Patrick died I had been smoking too much. The only time when I wasn't stoned was when I sat in Dr Hildebrand's office; it was one of his conditions. The Welsh police had inadvertently done me a good turn: without my home-grown I would have to sober up.

When I got back to the Tower I didn't feel quite so sanguine. Of course it was raining and the house was strangely run-down. In the end I'd stayed in Greece for three weeks and during that time it was obvious that the gardener hadn't been. The weather had been alternately sunny and wet so the garden had turned back into a wilderness. Yvette hadn't been either; dirty crockery filled the sink, beds were in disarray and Molly had clearly tried on and discarded several outfits. She went in for feather boas, chiffons and silks and her clothes were strewn around the floor and on the furniture, making the place look like a chorus girl's dressing-room.

I tidied up and rang Yvette. She sounded embarrassed and said she would come and see me. The gardener didn't have a phone.

In the morning, at the police station, I had my photograph and my fingerprints taken. The officer-in-charge told me that a date for my trial would be set for the following month.

George came down for a few days' fishing and Molly reappeared. She got rather drunk at dinner and I suggested that she stay the night.

'I'll make you up a bed on the first floor,' I said. Molly looked at me as if I was mad.

'Listen, girl,' she said, 'you haven't got the picture. *I'm* with George now.' At this point, George shuffled to his feet, said goodnight and went up the stairs to bed. 'You've lost your child,' she continued, 'and you're about to lose your husband, so go back to your mental home, we're selling the Tower.' And with that she followed George up to his room.

I went to bed furious. I thought I knew George well enough to realise that Molly's ambition hadn't come to much more than a romp in the bedroom, but I was angry that she had got rid of Yvette and the gardener and I was hurt that she had betrayed my friendship. Sleep was impossible, and it didn't help that I had to get up early to keep an appointment with a solicitor to discuss my defence. The realisation that I could get a prison sentence was beginning to sink in. I must have drifted off, because I woke to the sound of Molly shouting and George whispering in the kitchen. I flung open my door and shouted, 'Fuck off, fuck off out of my house.' George ran out of the back door saying that he was going fishing; Molly ran after him.

It was early autumn. A heavy, low-lying mist had come down in the night and as they ran through it across the field, with Molly gaining on George, all I could see were the two scuttling figures, visible only from the waist up.

CHAPTER 27

From Fat Wales to Thin Wales

Molly had told quite a few people about her plans. She had rung Francis to ask him if I could have a room in his house, and when he had said that there wasn't a spare one, she suggested a space could be made for me under his stairs. Marilyn, George's secretary, told me that George had been dreading my return and had been hoping that Molly would somehow magically disappear. After seeing my solicitor I went back to Wales on the train the same day, wondering if they would both be there and worried as to what the situation really was.

It was dark when I arrived. George was sitting at the kitchen table with a bottle of whisky and there was no sign of Molly. He was very contrite, not because he'd been to bed with her a few times, but because of what she had made of it. 'She's a good sort, really,' he said. I didn't agree.

At the end of August I had to appear in the magistrates' court. Mysteriously, I was only charged with about half the number of plants that I'd been growing. On the day, Bernie

Simons, my solicitor, came down to hold my hand. Anne Wollheim, Jasper Conran and Bruce were staying with me. Jasper, deciding that I probably would not be sent to prison, was going to cook lobster thermidor for lunch.

I stood in the dock while Bernie handed my psychiatric report to the magistrates and I was fined £250. It was on the local news and in the papers the next day. The caption read, 'Jazz musician's wife grows her own.' *The Times* published a very flattering photo of me, taken at least twenty years before.

After the trial, Anne thought I should have a brandy and offered me some of Bruce's, but Bruce wouldn't allow it, saying as it was only a tiny bottle, and Jasper would need it all for the lobster. I had some cooking brandy, so I swallowed some of that and then was sick in the garden while I was getting in the salad for lunch.

George wasn't able to be with us as he was on tour, but he received two letters saying what a wonderful wife I must be, 'prepared to take the rap for her husband'.

I loved having Jasper to stay and now that he and Bruce were a serious couple they were always there together. Jasper would arrive in his white sports car while Bruce anxiously paced the lane if he was late. Bruce scribbled away on the top floor and Jasper pushed the furniture to the side in another room, spread large sheets of paper all over the floor and designed his next collection. They had two complaints, heating and light: they said there weren't any angle-poise lamps and the house was too cold. I pointed out that there was a shop in Brecon that sold the former and perhaps they could wear something more suitable for the country than their skimpy T-shirts.

When Bruce went off to Australia to research *The Song Lines,* Jasper would often stay with me in London. He disapproved of my sloppy appearance, and if I went to meet him at his show-room he would dump what I had on in the bin and I would return home wearing some beautifully cut garment. I still have a lovely black satin, calf-length, pleated skirt, now old and much too tight round the waist for me, but not for Candy.

For Christmas Jasper gave me a drawing he'd done of a greenhouse filled with exotic climbing flowers. I thought it was just a pretty card, but the next day a lorry arrived with the real thing and a man to erect it.

That same year the stretch of river that George rented for fishing came up for sale. We went to the auction expecting it to go for £10,000 and that we might have to sell a picture. It went for £46,000 and we had to sell the lot. Without the fishing, George would not have wanted to keep the Tower and, standing on its own, surrounded by fields where an unfriendly farmer kept his sheep and cattle, it would be much harder to find a buyer. We would also have lost the right even to walk to the river. Anyway, it had always been George's dream to own some fishing, and he let his pictures go with hardly a sigh. We went out to celebrate with Bruce, who raised his glass. 'To the Lord of the Flowing Waters,' he said. George corrected him: 'To the Lord of the Empty Walls.'

When the miners went on strike in 1984, it was inevitable that, living so near the Welsh mining valleys, we would become involved. George did concerts with local bands to raise money for the food fund and I helped out at a large shed in Abertillery with the miners' wives where we distributed food parcels. Those early days were all full of optimism. Our food centre collected goods for 4,000 parcels each week: 4,000 loaves, tins of baby food, baked beans, corned beef, bags of sugar and cans of Cow & Gate baby milk. Everything was stored on the first floor because the ground floor was damp. The vans from the various pits would park at the front and several women would form a chain down the stairs, handing the carrier bags down until they reached the drivers.

I also emptied the house of all the endless bric-à-brac I'd collected over twenty-five years and took it to sell at the local antique shops. The money was welcome. Less so were the muddy vegetables from my garden.

Perhaps it was obvious to some that the strike could not succeed, but its failure only seemed possible to me when, tragically, a taxi-driver was killed on the M4. A striking miner had dropped a large brick from a bridge and it had gone through a man's windscreen. Sympathy began to turn, winter came, money was running out and the trickle back to work began. In March the strike was over and nearly all the mines in our valley would be closed, but at least the women had discovered strengths and organisational skills that they hadn't known they possessed.

CHAPTER 28

James Sebastian Fox

I remained friends with Beryl, one of the miners' wives, and in the spring, following the collapse of the strike, she rang me up about a fox cub. While walking on the hills she had come across a dead vixen and curled up beside its body were two cubs, not more than a few days old. She could raise one; could I raise the other?

It arrived in a small cardboard box and to stop it whimpering I carried it round in my apron pocket. We called him James Sebastian, James after James Fox the writer and Sebastian after Tom's best friend. At first James was fed on milk and water but soon progressed from mashed-up worms to tinned puppy food; minced liver he also loved, and chicken he would kill for.

His appearance at first was confusing to strangers – was it a kitten or a puppy, they would ask, and on being told his identity most people would be enthralled at being so close to a small wild animal.

His litter tray lived under the sink and he only had to be

shown its use once. In the wild he would have had to learn everything very quickly, and from his mother. As I was *in loco parentis* he thought he had to copy me. On the one occasion when he peed on the floor he mimicked me wiping it up, and he soon learned to open the fridge.

If I went to London on the train I would wear a cotton top that had a front pocket and James would snuggle down inside it. In London he liked to sleep in a cupboard between George's bedroom and his bathroom. When George got up to pee in the night, James would rush out and indulge in a little playful ankle-biting. He tolerated George and Tom, but on the whole he was frightened of men but not of women.

James took up all my time, and it was just as well that Lewis had finally vanished. And vanished completely. For two years his appearances had become more and more infrequent and then they just stopped. I knew that he no longer found me attractive, and sex with me had become difficult. When a photograph of me had appeared in the local paper during the strike, Lewis had seen it and said, 'God, do I really have a girlfriend that old?'

His last posting had been to France, and when I rang the number of his rented house I was informed by the operator that the line was discontinued. I wasn't really sorry. A month after the strike collapsed I'd gone with him to France for a few days and on the boat, where we played an endless boy-game called battleships, I ate some fish that turned my stomach to water. After a night of explosive diarrhoea and endless vomiting, the noises of which easily penetrated the thin wall between the bathroom and bedroom, I saw a look of revulsion on Lewis's face the next morning.

The week was not a success. I was quite pleased to go home, and soon after that, James arrived.

He grew up very quickly, but without siblings to play with or his mother to teach him, I was manoeuvred into the role of instructing him in the skills he would need for survival. I had never considered his future; I just assumed that I would care for him while he was a cub and then he would be old enough to cope on his own. That he would need lessons in catching food had not occurred to me. He made his needs quite clear: around ten at night he would wake up and lead me into the garden to play jump and catch. A cuddly teddy bear was cast as a chicken, which I would hurl into the air and James would leap after it. It was a cold wet spring and jump and catch went on for at least two hours every night. I began to worry about his future.

The Tower was going to be let to some fishermen for two weeks in June. Since we had bought the river I was able to make money by letting the house with the fishing when George was on tour. But now, two weeks in London with James presented a problem. We couldn't play jump and catch in our patio garden. In the end it wasn't too bad. We only stayed in London for two days and then I took him to a cottage in Sussex belonging to Arabella Boxer. Her cottage was in the middle of some woods, and James loved his new surroundings. He slept on my bed and was meticulous about using his litter tray. One afternoon when we were deep in the woods and James was learning to dig for worms, a family with a dog arrived. The dog barked and James shot off. I searched for hours and returned to Arabella and the cottage in despair. Finally I rang my friend Beryl, who suggested that I wait until dusk and then return to the spot where he had vanished. 'He'll come to you, don't worry,' she said. The wood was very quiet and dark. I wasn't even sure that I was in the right place, but I sat on a tree trunk and called softly. Suddenly, and quite silently, he was in front of me and then he jumped into my arms. His re-appearance had a magical quality, like a conjuring trick – one minute there was an empty space and then he was standing in it. We walked back to Arabella and the cottage and I finally realised the implications of loving and caring for a wild animal.

I had heard of an animal sanctuary near Bath, and when I rang them they said they would care for him in a less domestic environment until he was more independent.

Caroline Blackwood was writing a book about hunting and, for research purposes, she offered to come with me. It was the one hot day of the year and James behaved badly in the car. Caroline was nervous of James and that made him nervous too. He gave her a little nip and had to be shut up in his basket.

When we arrived at 'Bright and Beautiful', as the sanctuary was called, we were unable at first to find anyone. I let James out of his basket, opened the car window an inch and we set off down a track to a farmhouse. There were some sad-looking ponies in a field and we could hear dogs barking. At the farm house an ancient hippy greeted us and followed us back to the car. James had gone. I couldn't think how he had escaped. The inch of window didn't seem even large enough for his paw, but I realised he'd heard the dogs barking and had panicked. I called for a while but the dogs were now barking even more loudly and I knew he wouldn't come. The hippy suggested that we should come back in the evening, when the dogs would be in the house and silent. We got into the car and I started the engine. There was a scrabbling sound from behind the foot pedals and there was James, who had burrowed through the carpet and almost into the engine. It had not been an auspicious beginning. I had to leave him in a rather dirty shed and we drove off to find dinner and a B&B.

The Bath agricultural show was on and finding a B&B was difficult. Eventually the restaurant, where we drank two bottles of wine, booked us in with a Colonel and Mrs Powell. It was an elegant house with many china ornaments and several no-smoking signs. In the corner cupboard of our bedroom, amongst the shepherdesses, Caroline found a pretty bowl that she decided would serve as an ashtray. She lay in bed smoking and I lay in bed worrying. By morning I had decided to go back to Bright and Beautiful and rescue James. Mrs Powell waited on us at breakfast. Caroline was still smoking and kept slopping her orange juice on to the large, shiny dining table. Mrs Powell kept leaping forward and setting the glass back on the place mat which Caroline had ignored. We left to go and I let Caroline pay the bill as I knew her title would appear on the cheque and it might be some consolation to the Colonel and his wife.

When I was 100 yards from James's shed, he heard or smelt me and started calling. The relief of knowing that he wouldn't have to spend another night at Dotheboy's Hall was immense, but his future was still unsettled.

I now had a month before the Tower was let again and in that time I had to find a solution. Someone had told me that Miriam Rothschild had moved on to foxes from fleas when, aged eighty, her failing eyesight had made her study of the latter impractical. We spoke on the phone and she explained that her tennis courts had been fenced in for her foxes. Some were young and some were old or injured. James would be welcome. But I must come too. She had a cottage on the estate where I could live until James was used to his new home. Would my domestic situation allow me to take advantage of this? I didn't think it would, a decision that I later regretted. But I made other enquiries and decided to take up the offer that a forester in Ludlow had made. He had a large deer pen, full of rabbits, grubs and worms, and there

James could live until he improved his survival skills. Also, Christopher the forester would make sure that at first there was always some food for him.

It was raining when we left the Tower and as I drove to Ludlow I felt some relief that I wouldn't be playing jump and catch at midnight. James had formed an attachment to my slippers and I left them in the pen with him. Christopher said that I could ring and check on his progress. I did ring, I rang often. But every day I minded more and missed him more. Finally, when I heard that he had dug himself out of the pen and was gone, I thought my heart would break.

CHAPTER 29

Kevin and Tracy

One evening I went down to George's rooms to mend his bedside light. Leaning against his desk was a youngish woman in a very short mini. I assumed she was a friend of Candy's, but when George asked me *why* I was going to *his* bedroom, I realised that she must be a new girlfriend, and that he wanted her to know I didn't share his room.

Later that evening, he told me that they had only just met. She had been sitting at the next table in our local restaurant and had leant across and eaten off his plate. It was the beginning of an affair that at times seemed likely to end our marriage.

At the time, 1985, she was in her late thirties, but her high-pitched little girlie voice and her style of dressing made her seem younger. I called her 'the Greckel' because Emma Tennant told me about a bird of that name; it lived on one of the Caribbean islands and caused a lot of distress with its unpleasant screeching. George was enthralled by her: she was upper-class, she drank, was outrageous, sexually wild and even needier than I had ever been. I was frightened of her. She seemed to represent a manipulative and destructive side of me that I hoped I had abandoned.

People told me tales about her uninhibited behaviour, which made George's excesses sound mild by comparison.

Greckel had her fans, but the majority of our friends disliked her, and when the affair had been going on for some months and George told me that Greckel didn't feel that I made her welcome in the house, I was confident enough to say that, as far as I was concerned, she wasn't.

George had his own sitting-room next to his bedroom and also a tiny kitchenette. Alongside the kettle in this room appeared two grey mugs. On one was written 'Kevin' and on the other 'Tracy'. I hated this mixture of pet names and snobbishness.

If, after Patrick died, our marriage had been difficult, it now became unfriendly and all the bridges that had been half-mended began to sag. George said that I must let him know if I was coming to London from Wales, so that Greckel would have the option of not being in the house at the same time as I was. Once I had come back to find that Pandora and a friend were in the rooms above me, and Greckel and George in his rooms below. Initially Pandora had been befriended by Greckel, but something had gone wrong and lately, if she came to the house, she was not encouraged to be downstairs in George's rooms. In fact, George said to me, rather pompously I thought, 'I'm having a very important affair, and I would prefer it if Pandora wasn't around when Greckel is.'

When summer came, I was happy to be in Wales and not sandwiched between George's girlfriend and his daughter. That autumn both Candy and Tom were almost living at the Tower, Tom because he had an acting job in Cardiff and could often commute, and Candy because she had let her London studio flat and was working as a bar-maid in Brecon. And then in January she told me that she was pregnant. At first I was thrilled: she was twenty-five, I didn't know the father was already married and she was glowing with happiness. When I realised that she would be a single mother, I became anxious and tried to persuade her to go to the Pregnancy Advisory Service who I thought would help her to have an abortion. But Candy knew she wanted to have the baby and I have always been glad that she didn't take my advice. More than glad.

Once the fishing season started in March, George came down as often as he could. In May he had two clear weeks' holiday and I looked forward to him coming and to starting on the bridge-building again. Wales was always good for us both.

The morning after he arrived the phone rang. We both picked it up in separate rooms and I said to George, who was now very deaf, 'Don't worry, I've got it.' A voice said, 'This is the *Sunday* . . . Mr Melly, we wanted to ask you about your love child.' I put the receiver down and went into the garden, not worried because I assumed they had just discovered Pandora, now twenty-five years old and not even a love child.

I was making an elaborate raised bed for the carrots in order to thwart the carrot fly, when George came stumbling out. 'I've been meaning to tell you,' he said – and then I heard the whole story.

Before Greckel, he had been having an affair with a young woman who had just had a child, and although George was not her only lover he was a possible father.

If Candy had not been pregnant, I would have left George then. But Candy was pregnant, five months, and her situation was not dissimilar. She had also wanted a child, but unlike George's friend, she hadn't known that the father was married, and when she found out it was too late, she had fallen in love. The father was an office manager called David and lived a few miles from Brecon. Not only was he married, but when he started the affair with Candy his wife was six months' pregnant. I didn't think I would make him any more welcome in the house than Greckel; I hated seeing Candy so unhappy. Sometimes I would drive her into Brecon to meet him. She would hang around in the carpark and when he failed to turn up would ring for me to fetch her home.

George went back to London early – I wasn't speaking to him – and Candy, trying to break with her lover, went back to London with George. I sat in a rage by myself.

When Tom was about four years old my father had watched him playing and had said, 'He's about the same age as your little half-brother – don't think I ever mentioned him.' I hadn't replied, but I never stopped thinking about it. If it was true, my father had gone on having affairs long after he'd left my mother and one of these women had a child, a child that looked like my son. I found it unbearable. That possible half-brother (I didn't even know if my father was telling the truth) and Candy's future baby, and now this other baby, a possible half-sister to Tom, all contributed to my confusion and unhappiness – and my anger.

I fell ill with bronchitis, I didn't answer the phone and it wasn't until George's sister Andrée wrote to me from Ibiza, where she had gone to live, that I was able to accept the situation. Her letter was loving, but she also pointed out how often George had stuck by me when I had been in trouble and needed him. After all, I was looking forward to Candy's baby, George's girlfriend had decided to live with one of the putative fathers and would not be seeing George again, therefore he would not be seeing the baby – so what did I have to be jealous of.

Greckel was also proving to be rather a handful. She had gone round the house, emptied it of all the pills she could find and got into bed with George, saying, 'I just want to die in your arms.' George called the ambulance and got her to hospital. When I told Anne Wollheim the story she said, 'What a pity he'd understood her. If he'd heard, "I just want to *lie* in your arms" he wouldn't have called the ambulance.'

Although Candy had not been able to break with David she had come back to live at the Tower to wait for the baby. In Brecon she attended baby classes and once, ironically enough, she had been handed David's three-month-old baby to bathe. But Candy didn't see much of David in the last weeks of her pregnancy. Perhaps he was helping his wife with her baby, or perhaps he just didn't fancy pregnant women.

In the middle of September, when the baby was already two weeks late, we had an exotic visitor, Peter Langan. With Michael Caine and the chef, Richard Shepherd, Peter owned

Langan's, a fashionable restaurant in Mayfair. Peter was often drunk and nearly always charming. He was very Irish and usually wore a crumpled white suit, which, in Tangier during the war, would have made him look at home. His arrival had been threatened since August, when George was on holiday and Peter had announced his intention of fishing with him. But George had gone back on tour and only Tom and a friend of his called Sarah were on hand to help with Peter, should he arrive.

His secretary rang one day and told us that he would be arriving on a particular train and would take a taxi from the station. Although we had all been looking forward to a diversion from the anxiety of waiting for the baby, we were also relieved when he didn't show up. Just before lunch the next day we heard a taxi bumping down the drive. It was a London taxi and from it emerged a rather drunk Peter and a bemused driver. Apparently Peter had missed all the trains from Paddington, but had persuaded a taxi driver to bring him straight to the Tower. Unfortunately Peter had lost the address and their route had taken them on a tour of Wales which lasted fifteen hours.

Tom and Sarah took him off to explore the local pubs and were enormously impressed by the amount of draught cider, Irish whiskey and champagne he could drink.

That night, after dinner, when several bottles of wine had been consumed, Peter hauled himself up to bed. I had made him promise to be quiet, explaining that Candy needed her sleep, as she could be in labour at any moment. Peter asserted that he knew all about confinements and he bet a case of champagne that the baby's birth was not imminent.

The noise of an amorous Peter trying to break into Sarah's room, which she was sharing with Candy, was the first thing to wake me. The second thing was Peter stumbling about in the kitchen and breaking the top off a bottle of wine, having failed to find a corkscrew. I snatched it off him and poured it down the sink. Peter collapsed at the bottom of the stairs. Tom and I dragged him up to his room and threw him on the bed.

He came down the next morning looking none the worse, and he was muttering, as he looked at my grim face, 'Poor George, poor George.' After breakfast he went into Brecon and bought a ten-pound salmon in the market and wrote in George's fishing book, 'September 20th, 10 lb salmon, caught on a fly by Peter Langan'.

It was a hot, sunny September and we had lunch in the garden. Peter left soon afterwards, and eight days later Kezzie was born. Peter sent the champagne.

Kezzie was born in Brecon and I was able to watch the unfailing miracle of birth. I often looked after Kezzie during the day, and now that Candy had rented a little house in Brecon, I had Kezzie for the night if Candy wanted to go out with her friends.

George and I had patched things up enough for us all to spend Christmas at the Tower. Only the lovers were missing: David, Kezzie's father, was with his family in Brecon, Lewis was now only a humiliating memory, and Greckel was presumably somewhere in the shires. There were two reasons why I never quizzed George about her: one, I didn't want my hatred and fear fed by detail, and two, it was easier to forget her if she remained in the shadows.

Only one thing upset the Christmas goodwill: George set fire to Patrick's shrub. I had asked him to take the rubbish down to the pond, but as far away from the shrub as possible, and burn it in the incinerator. Patrick's ashes had come in a coffin-shaped, shiny, wooden box and this I had buried in a spot near the pond. On top I had planted a buddleia because it flowered in June and his birthday was that month. George had mis-heard me and stood the incinerator right next to the shrub. I should have known that George was unable to compensate for his deafness with anything like common sense. There was a stiff breeze and the Christmas wrappings, along with the buddleia, went up in smoke.

CHAPTER 30

George Gets Shrunk

Although I had finished my course of bereavement counselling (leaving Dr Hildebrand with an incomplete video tape), the Tavi had kept in touch with me and I went for a follow-up session shortly after Kezzie was born. Dr Hildebrand, who was rather dismayed by the state of my marriage, offered me family counselling. This would either have to mean all of us, or just me and George.

Understandably, Candy didn't fancy travelling up to London each week with a three-month-old baby to discuss, amongst other things, her relationship with David. Tom was keen, but without Candy and Kezzie it had to be just me and George.

As a couple we were allotted two counsellors and the second one was called Mrs Wise. There were several reasons why George found therapy difficult: one was his increasing deafness coupled with Mrs Wise's quiet, gentle voice, and the other was his ability to turn any remark or incident into a joke. He commented that the noisy builders in the next-door house had been sent by Jung. Dr Hildebrand did not appreciate George's 'joke work' and gave a very faint smile. Perhaps the only thing that the two men had in common was their inability to use a machine: Dr Hildebrand's video camera refused to record our sessions.

George and I would have lunch afterwards at a Chinese restaurant in the Finchley Road, and I felt friendlier towards him – perhaps the Tavi was helping. But Greckel was still a large part of his life and causing constant dramas. It was obvious to me (if not to him) that she would not be content until she lived with him. Although I would spend a night or two in London each week, I was more often in Wales helping Candy with Kezzie. Greckel must have thought she was nearly home.

But George has a strong sense of loyalty, a conservative dislike of change, and he still loved me. Once the fishing season started he came down to Wales whenever he could. Greckel often rang when he was there, sometimes in the middle of the night. One minute he would say that Greckel was too difficult and that he must finish with her; the next day he would suggest that she should move in with him. In London, George's bedroom and sitting-room were on the lower ground floor with French windows on to a split-level patio garden. He thought that half of that space could be covered in and made into a small kitchen. Would I facilitate this plan? No, I would not.

In May, when Kezzie was eight months old, I took her for a week to stay in Corfu where a friend had a house on the sea. While I was there Candy rang to tell me that George had been in hospital for twenty-four hours but was now home.

Greckel was looking after him and there was nothing to worry about.

By the time I got home George was back on the road. Kidney stones had been diagnosed and then passed. I took Kezzie back to Wales and there George rang me. He wanted a divorce, he wanted to live with Greckel, I must stay in Wales until things were arranged. I wandered round the house and then into the garden. I walked up to the village to see Yvette, who was still working for me. She made me some strong tea with lots of sugar, which she said was good for shock. I felt very sick when I walked back down the lane, and rather frightened. I thought that I'd only got what I deserved: she was there and I was not, she slept with him and I did not, she laughed at his jokes and I did not. I saw that someone had left me a message on my answerphone. It was George. He'd changed his mind and was coming down to fish that weekend.

For a short while he stopped seeing Greckel, but by the autumn in 1987 their affair was full-on again and I began to plan to bring things to a head. I decided that in the New Year I would go to India and take Tom. Greckel was not the only reason, there were two others: Tom had been very depressed for nearly a year and his depression triggered very violent headaches. The third reason was Candy and Kezzie. I felt that she needed time to be alone with her daughter. A grandmother permanently on call was not necessarily in anyone's best interests. She now had a wide circle of friends in Brecon, many of whom had young children too, and Yvette said that she would have Kezzie one day a week.

Once it was established that Tom's headaches had no physical cause, I bought *The Rough Guide to India* and began to plan. Andrée's daughter, my niece Natasha, was working in London and I was able to let our rooms to her and a friend. This would help our budget, which was £100 a week. We planned to stay for three months and spend all our time in the South. Using buses, trains and finding cheap rooms, I thought our budget was ample. Also the Tower was let to a young couple who were house-hunting in the area, and as our time in India corresponded with the closed fishing season, George would not want to be there.

We had our jabs and I made endless lists, but there was one thing I wanted to do. Earlier that year I had gone with Jasper Conran to see Bruce in France. Bruce had been ill for a couple of years. All the signs pointed to AIDS. He was staying in Shirley Conran's house near Grasse, a château really, with lofty rooms, a large roof terrace and crumbling stone steps which led down to the village. In spite of the creature comforts, it was an uncomfortable visit. Bruce, who in the past had almost separated from his wife, had eventually left Jasper and gone back to Elizabeth the previous year. Jasper had been very hurt.

Bruce came rather shakily down the steps to meet us. He was leaning on a stick and his face had the tell-tale black blotches of AIDS. That night Elizabeth fetched a camp bed and placed it across the threshold of Bruce's room for her to sleep on. Jasper was furious: 'Does she think I'm going to leap on him in the night?'

The next day we drove to Monte Carlo for lunch. Jasper took my arm and we walked ahead of Bruce and Elizabeth.

Bruce would have liked to catch up with us, but we were walking too quickly for him. Jasper had made his point. Bruce had made his choice and must live – and die – with it.

We flew back the next day. 'Do you think it's really AIDS?' I asked him on the plane. 'Not if he says it isn't,' replied Jasper.

That visit had been in January and now, ten months later, I wanted to see Bruce again. The rumour surrounding his illness had mushroomed and it was hard to believe that anything other than AIDS could account for his symptoms. I booked my flight, but the day before my departure Elizabeth rang to say that Bruce had gone into hospital and could not have any visitors.

It was therapy day for me and George, and I was crying in the taxi on the way to the Tavi. George thought the tears were about some misdemeanour of his, and kept saying to Dr Hildebrand and Mrs Wise, 'I don't know what I've done.' When I explained that it was because I thought Bruce was dying, our therapists suggested that George should try to comfort me. 'I don't know how to any more,' he said. He put his arm round my shoulders, and we sat there, rather stiffly, while the therapist explained to George that not only would he soon be missing me, as I was leaving any day for Bombay, but he would also be missing his therapists. He didn't look very convinced.

APART FROM TOM'S suffering from a large infestation of worms, India was a success. We didn't quarrel, only Tom's Filofax was stolen and when we got fed up with each other we went in different directions for a few days, Tom into the hills while I explored the temple cities.

George wrote that the Greckel had had a breakdown and was staying with her shrink. 'She is so sad,' he wrote, 'but I really just can't dump her at her lowest, and I'm fond of her too. No doubt it will work itself out in the end.'

We were back at the Tower in March. Candy and Kezzie were thrilled to have us home and we all looked forward to Easter, when George would be coming down for two weeks to fish.

One morning I came in from tidying the shed – one of my favourite jobs – to hear the phone ringing. It was almost a year since George had rung to say that he wanted a divorce, and it seemed that the Tavi, India and the last year hadn't happened: he repeated his wish to leave me and live with Greckel.

He suggested that Tom and I should stay in Wales as Greckel was in the London house. Greckel had once rather liked Tom and given him an alarm clock in the unlikely shape of Superman, a hero Tom much admired. But she could be very contrary and she seemed to have gone off him.

Days passed. Candy came over with Kezzie, Yvette commiserated and made lots of sweet tea and we were all very quiet and careful of each other. At night I lay in bed and made plans: where to live, what to sell, what to do. Plans keep feelings at bay.

George's phone call was on a Friday and on the following Tuesday he rang to say he hadn't meant it. Greckel had been upset about him coming to the Tower for two weeks and he'd found himself saying things he regretted. He would have rung before, but he'd been in Manchester over the weekend and hadn't had time. He hoped I hadn't been too upset.

George was going to be sixty-two that year, I would be fifty-one, we had been married (to each other) for twenty-seven years. In spite of our different enthusiasms, our separate lives and our separate beds, I couldn't imagine a life without him. Apparently he felt the same.

CHAPTER 31

Technophobia

George has never been very practical. At Christmas I am the one to get an electric screwdriver while George gets a silk shirt. His inability to cope with any domestic problem, with or without a screwdriver, coupled with his deafness, has made it difficult for him to organise his life and his complicated arrangements for travelling around the country to sing and lecture. He would phone me in Wales and say he must hurry as he was catching a train to Devon.

'No, that's tomorrow.'

'No, Diana, today, Friday, it's in your handwriting in my diary.'

'But today is Thursday.'

'Are you sure?'

'Quite sure.'

It was also difficult for him to be in Wales on his own. Usually, if I had to go to London I would just go up for the day. The first time I did leave him he scalded himself on the kettle steam and set the smoke alarm off with burnt toast. He

205

rang to ask me how to stop the noise of the alarm, and then forgot to replace the receiver. Unable to phone him back, I rang Yvette and asked her to go down to deal with everything. That night when I got back, George told me that while she was there, Yvette had taken a bed and breakfast booking for two 'humans', who would be arriving before ten o'clock. The 'humans' turned out to be Germans.

I had started doing 'Bed and Breakfast at the Tower' soon after Kezzie was born. Her arrival had meant that I was more often in Wales, where she and Candy were living, than in London. Although I still let the Tower with the fishing on a self-catering basis, B&B was more convenient and it was something that I was good at.

My mother had started doing B&B when we moved to West Mersea in Essex after the war. We had a small house near the sea and during the summer I slept in a tent in the garden and the room that I shared with my brother was given to 'guests'. In the morning I would take Tuppy for a run on the beach and then help my mother set the table for the breakfasts before I went to school. The house belonged to an elderly lady who had the other best bedroom and whom my mother looked after. When she died she left my mother the house. We sold it and bought a larger house, further from the sea but nearer to 'The Hard', where all the sailing boats were moored. Here my mother hoped to attract a better class of customer. She did, but unfortunately this venture coincided with my father's demob. Once out of the Air Force he was unable to find a job and became drunk and unhappy. This was the beginning of my mother's depression; perhaps she also missed 'Uncle Guy'. My brother was away at boarding school (probably paid for by our paternal grandfather), and not able to help, but I often truanted from school, much preferring to make beds and cook breakfast for our 'guests' than learn chemistry. I could say I was one of those children who loved history, English and art but hated the sciences. I didn't, I hated them all.

My B&B customers loved the Tower and not least because George was often there at the same time, sharing the breakfast table with them. Not everyone recognised him, particularly if they came from abroad, but they all responded to his eccentric appearance and didn't seem to mind that he never seemed to hear a single thing they said.

I had first noticed that George was deaf on our honeymoon; on the long drive to Scotland, he couldn't hear the cigarette lighter pop out from its hole. But now, twenty-five years later and with a good hearing-aid, he made many curious muddles. The band kept a notebook of 'George's deafies' and I dealt with them, sometimes patiently but more often not. George dealt with it in his most typical fashion: rather than make an intelligent guess at what might have been said, he preferred to make a humorous one. This could be infuriating, and I began to seriously hate all jokes.

Being so deaf, and also needing stronger glasses, meant that he often lost or mislaid things: cheques, keys, bank-cards, rail tickets and letters. When the post arrived George's idea of sorting was to put everything in a tidy pile. As long as the pile looked neat, cheques could go in the bin and letters for any other family member would be buried along with all the urgent contracts and faxes.

Faxes were another hurdle. Our own fax number was

written on the machine. This confused George, who, when trying to send a fax, would inevitably dial his own number, only to find it permanently engaged. Once he rang me in Wales to say that my old travelling companion, Penelope Tree, had sent me a fax from Australia. 'Could you fax it to me here?' I asked. 'But it already *is* a fax,' he said, rather baffled.

Sometimes his failing hearing and eyesight could make him stubborn and paranoid. One night in Wales, unable to find his torch, which he would need while stumbling back from the river in the dark, he borrowed mine. 'Don't break it or lose it,' I said smugly. The next morning it had gone. George swore he'd put it on his writing table and pointed to an exact spot. He kept insisting that he *knew* that's what he did, and was *I* sure that *I* didn't absent-mindedly take it back. I pointed out that I was the one with all my faculties, even if I couldn't lecture on Surrealism, and if he'd put it there it would still be there. It was much the same kind of dialogue I used to have with the children over lost books and shoes. George sat on the bed with his kaftan on inside-out, looking dejected. We searched the room: did the cats take it to play with, did he use it while attempting (and failing) to change a light bulb, did I take it? I began to wonder. I suggested that he had his shower while I continued to search, but he wouldn't leave the room, clearly thinking that I would retrieve it from where I'd hidden it once his back was turned. Pockets were gone through, bed pulled to bits, waders shaken. The bed and breakfast guests offered to search the river path. But George knew he couldn't have crossed the field and got over the stile without it. 'Anyway,' he said

defiantly, banging his fist on the table, 'I put it right there.'
He then took his dressing-gown off a hook and there,
dangling innocently from its little black strap, was the torch.

'Now I remember,' he said triumphantly.

On the whole London was an easier house for him to
manage. The exception to this was when he was appearing at
Ronnie Scott's over Christmas. This was because Christmas
put him in a bad mood, and he always came home drunk.
Venetia said that he hated Christmas because it was someone
else's birthday; and for someone who expected his own to be
treated like the Queen's, it never occurred to him to
acknowledge anyone else's. He once came down to breakfast
at the Tower to find the kitchen table covered in cards and
parcels. It was my birthday and George, as usual, had
forgotten. 'What's all this stuff?' he demanded, rather
petulantly for him. 'There's no room for my breakfast.' One
of my presents was a tube of rather expensive chocolate
truffles. I kept them for the weekend, when friends were
coming. But when I got them out after dinner, the tube,
although empty, showed no sign of having been opened.
George confessed – he had attacked it from the bottom end
and taken two out each night after a disappointing evening
on the river. We had a very enjoyable row.

Christmas was the only time of the year when George got
grumpy and depressed, but not the only time he drank too
much, just the time when he drank the most. The season at
Ronnie Scott's was for three or four weeks, six nights a week,
ending at two a.m. George was enormously popular and
Ronnie's was packed every night with people wanting to buy
him a drink. Some nights he could pace himself, not because

he saw any harm in being drunk and behaving badly, but because he knew that although his performance was fuelled by alcohol, it could also be ruined by it.

Usually it was the long wait for the taxi after the show had ended that led to an extra half hour of hanging about, and three more large whiskies.

Sometimes when he came home he would fancy what he called a 'mixed grill', and he would stagger into the kitchen and fry up eggs and black pudding.

This treat was soon forbidden. The gas was often left on, frying pans were burnt and the entire household woken up. Deaf people are very noisy. The problem of George's late-night hunger pangs was never satisfactorily solved. In the downstairs study next to his bedroom was some basic kitchen equipment: a kettle, a small fridge and some cups and saucers (but not the Kevin and Tracy ones – I'd chucked those out).

George would have had a proper dinner before Ronnie's, and could always have had a 'mixed grill' in the interval. In the interests of safety and sanity it was decided that he would be confined to his own quarters when he came home. I did once say that he could go to the real kitchen if he was sober, but rather sensibly he pointed out that if he wasn't, he would be the last to know.

I stocked his little fridge with Covent Garden soups and cartons of milk. Unfortunately these cartons are somewhat similar – only somewhat, but George often complained that his cornflakes tasted of spring vegetable or tomato and basil. Also, not being a technical person, he didn't realise that the kettle had to be plugged in and switched on to function efficiently. I went down one morning to find out for him if it had fused. 'It got warm,' he said, 'but not hot.' I realised what had happened – he'd filled the kettle with warm water, but failed to plug it in.

Our marriage was changing, because I was changing. I had become a grandmother and even more of a martinet. Women friends would say, 'You're still a beautiful woman.' The 'still' says it all. It means you have left the sexual arena – in my case only too willingly. For the first ten years of marriage to George I put too much energy into being so attractive to him that he would not look away. When our uxorious relationship collapsed on that holiday in the South of France I became masochistically involved with unsuitable men. It was now my turn to indulge in a more caring role, and it was no wonder that I felt relief to be able to wear the invisible cloak that envelops most women over fifty.

CHAPTER 32

Bruce then Teddy

When Bruce Chatwin first knew he was ill he had rung me from Switzerland. He told me that he was dying and asked if I would be his literary executor.

I hadn't taken him seriously on either subject. I thought he was exaggerating his illness. I had seen him with a slight cold acting more like a man than an explorer, and I didn't realise how ill he was. I assumed I would die long before him and would not be obliged to fulfil his request, a role that I knew perfectly well I was not equipped for.

Two years later I was driving down to see Bruce with Francis Wyndham. Bruce, now reconciled to his wife, Elizabeth, was in bed at their house near Oxford. During the drive Francis and I discussed the possible cause of his illness and whether it was or wasn't AIDS. Perhaps we both preferred to believe it was an illness from which Bruce could recover. In 1988 it wasn't usual for people to live long with AIDS.

I told Francis about my dilemma concerning Bruce's

request for me to be his literary executor. To bring it up if he was dying didn't seem very tactful. Luckily Bruce solved the problem. When we arrived he was lying in bed, just able to cross the floor with the help of Elizabeth and confidently talking about a journey he was planning to some far-off place I'd never heard of, which seemed to involve camping and a donkey. Over lunch he brought up the subject of his literary executor; and he asked Francis if it could be him. Francis explained that as he was so much older, he didn't feel it was appropriate, and he suggested Susannah Clapp. Susannah had been Bruce's editor on several occasions and he loved the idea. He rang Susannah at once and she accepted.

Bruce didn't go on his donkey journey, but instead went back to Shirley Conran's house near Grasse. Shirley is a generous woman and was pleased to have Bruce and Elizabeth as her guests, but she had another reason for wanting Bruce out of England. Jasper was now making clothes for Princess Di and as this was before the Princess's sympathy for AIDS patients was known, there was a risk that any link the paparazzi might make could be detrimental to her son's career.

The winter following my visit to Bruce with Francis, I got a phone call from Teddy Millington-Drake. Ever since Bruce had taken me to stay on Patmos during the Molly Parkin era, Teddy and I had remained good friends. He rang from Italy to say that he had just been to see Bruce and that we must go soon as Bruce could not live long.

Francis, George and I booked our tickets for the next weekend.

The timing wasn't good: Candy and Kezzie were staying

with me in London and Candy had a bad chest infection. Tom was in Switzerland, au pairing for another family, and so there was no one to look after Kezzie.

I had booked a nanny for the weekend, but there would be a short gap between our leaving and the nanny's arrival. Tom's girlfriend reluctantly agreed to fill in for the hour.

When we arrived at the château, Shirley bustled us on to the terrace, offered champagne and told us not to touch Bruce as even a finger lightly stroking him would hurt.

Bruce had just had a two-hour examination by the doctor, who was now talking to Elizabeth. Also present was a young man with black hair and blue eyes who turned out to be a homeopathic doctor from Devon. We all went into Bruce's room; he was lying asleep on a large bed in a room off the terrace. Shirley and Elizabeth had a short quarrel about where an orchid should be placed. Shirley wanted it where Bruce could see it, on a shelf over a radiator, Elizabeth thought the heat would kill it. Shirley said she was going to her room with the doctor and, if we wanted her, to go on to the terrace and ring the hand bell. She said that we would know if Bruce woke up as his breathing would alter slightly but his eyes would be open all the time. Elizabeth went to the chemist to get Bruce's medicine and also some shaving cream that the painter Derek Hill had asked her for; he said it could only be obtained in the Grasse area.

After half an hour Bruce's eyes became more focused and he seemed to be saying 'Birdie' and was quite agitated. I rang the hand bell for Shirley, who came down and said it meant pee bottle. She left. After a while it became obvious that Bruce's bed was soiled. I rang again and Shirley and I changed him. It was difficult moving him. After that I was alone with Bruce, who groaned every now and then. I began to feel anxious and puzzled. There was only a bottle of aspirin by his bed and Elizabeth's plan that she, Francis and I were to bring Bruce back to London, and that initially he should stay at our house, didn't seem realistic.

Later that evening I rang home. Candy was worse, but Kezzie was fine. George rang the chemist to see if they had tracked down the shaving cream (Derek had been very insistent). Elizabeth was worried there wasn't enough fish for dinner. Shirley was being conspiratorial, having finally finished her three-hour session with the doctor which turned out to have been a conference with the homeopathic one about her back.

Francis and George both said that they thought it out of the question to subject Bruce to the plane ride and then have him at our home. I agreed. I told Elizabeth, who said she had booked three seats for him on the plane, that he was only depressed and would be all right, and that there was nowhere else for him to go.

We all had our own huge suites complete with bathrobes, sewing kits, spare toothbrushes (just as well, as I'd forgotten mine), Biros, and the Grasse equivalent of Floris. George was feeling desperate: he couldn't find his suitcase. It finally turned up in a cupboard in one of his rooms that he had thought was a door to another room. Each suite had about a dozen doors in it. In fact, finding someone you wanted a quiet word with was difficult: you discovered that you'd been whispering someone's name outside what turned out to be a store cupboard or yet another bathroom.

I was designated to feed Bruce his supper. I sat on his bed and put a bit of dry salmon in his mouth. It stayed there. I took it out. Elizabeth came in and said he must eat. I said he wasn't hungry.

Shirley came in; Elizabeth went. Shirley started whispering to Bruce that he didn't really want to go to London but back to the nice nursing home near Cannes. I thought she said Kent and felt rather puzzled.

Shirley, George, Francis and I were all a little drunk after supper and I asked Elizabeth – Why was she bringing him back? And the explanation that she couldn't get proper doctors and nurses anywhere except in London made sense. We decided we would manage the plane ride between us and find somewhere suitable for him to stay.

MIDNIGHT: GEORGE HAS gone to bed and Elizabeth is with Bruce. Shirley, Francis and I are talking in Shirley's bedroom. It's very white and lacy, with no smoking. We move into Francis's room. Shirley goes on about the press meeting us at Heathrow and wants me to tell Elizabeth that I can't have Bruce at home. I say that we all think that Bruce should be got home to England but to hospital, not to our house.

Sunday: Elizabeth agrees that if possible Bruce can go to a London hospital. Many phone calls are made. The Lighthouse (AIDS hospice) isn't listed. Someone manages to find the number and we ring a Lighthouse doctor. Bruce's brother rings and keeps saying QED. I ring home. Candy's gone to hospital. The Lighthouse doctor rings back: he is finding a bed for Bruce. I ring Andrée: will she take over from the nanny on

Monday? Yes. I ring the nanny: Kezzie's fine. The Lighthouse doctor rings again. Elizabeth answers and says Bruce is much better. Shirley makes several calls. I try to ring the Lighthouse doctor to explain that Elizabeth is exhausted and Bruce isn't better. We don't want to lose the bed.

Twelve noon: on the terrace with more champagne. Bruce is pushed out on a stretcher to lie in the sun. Elizabeth cooks fish pie for the veggies, stew for George and a coddled egg for Bruce. He doesn't eat it, but sleeps peacefully all day. George and Francis and I all feel that he is fading. Every now and then Elizabeth tries to encourage him to speak or eat or swallow a pill. We are so relieved that his groaning has stopped, we wish she wouldn't.

Six o'clock: Elizabeth is going on about it being a better day. We disagree. Better for us but not really for him.

Eight o'clock: Shirley rings the local restaurant and orders huge meals. Elizabeth makes soup for Bruce and inexplicably puts a Christmas pudding on to steam which boils dry and burns the saucepan. Shirley makes cabbage and bacon, fennel salad and potatoes Lyonnaise. I ring BUPA's SOS number to see if Bruce is covered for air ambulance. He isn't. Elizabeth is therefore confronted with the possibility of Air France refusing to take Bruce. She says that isn't possible, they had agreed. I make a secret call to Air France, who say it is a last-minute and final decision by the pilot.

George throws away all the uneaten food and washes up.

I relieve Francis, who has been with Bruce who is groaning again and frightened of the face he sees. I tell him it's the pain and that it will soon go.

One o'clock a.m.: bed.

Two-thirty: Elizabeth comes in. Bruce is worse. She's phoned for the ambulance.

Three-thirty: it arrives. Shirley and I accompany Elizabeth and the stretcher as it's bumped down the endless cobbled steps to where the ambulance is parked. Bruce is given oxygen.

Next day: luckily Francis and George have slept through the night and are therefore still making sense. George rings the chemist about the shaving cream – the line is occupied. I ring home. Candy is being kept in hospital, some of her lung has collapsed.

Shirley packs up all Bruce and Elizabeth's things and we take a taxi to the hospital in Nice. Shirley goes into Bruce's room and comes out to tell us that we won't want to see him. Elizabeth looks defeated. I think she feels Bruce died when he left the château and she keeps saying she wants him off all life-support machines. He isn't on any, just oxygen.

Three o'clock: we find an open couscous café. George orders steak. Shirley talks to him about pottery but he doesn't hear one word. Elizabeth talks to Francis about her sheep. George draws Picassos on the paper tablecloth. Shirley tries to draw a Matisse on her bit.

Back to the hospital. George and I put on gowns and go into Bruce's room. My money belt is bulging with my ticket and passport under my T-shirt; the nurse congratulates me on an expected baby.

Bruce is being moved to another hospital. He's been in a light coma since morning. He is wheeled out past us all into the lift.

At the airport we cancel Bruce's seats.

Back home: Candy will be allowed out tomorrow. Andrée is sitting with a large whisky at the kitchen table: Kezzie took a shine to the Bayswater Road and walked her up and down it all afternoon.

TWO DAYS AFTER we left, Bruce died. It was January 1989. Four years later in the summer of 1993 Teddy Millington-Drake told me he was HIV positive. Those four years made a huge difference. I think there were many reasons why Bruce sometimes denied that he had AIDS: he was married, he would have minded his parents knowing and perhaps he just didn't want to believe it. Teddy was always openly gay and by the time he was diagnosed we had all become only too familiar with the illness. Most of us knew at least one person who had died. Princess Diana and Elizabeth Taylor had raised the public's awareness, and a diagnosis was now greeted with sadness rather than shocked incomprehension.

During Teddy's last summer he began to talk quite openly about dying. After he had been told to put on weight we went two or three times a week to restaurants. He had always been a 'picky' eater, but now each course was shuffled around the plate and then rejected. Teddy got thinner and thinner and I put on a stone, frequently eating his food as well as my own in order to avoid disappointing the waiters who, like so many people, had fallen for Teddy at first sight.

There were dreaded visits to the Chelsea & Westminster Hospital for blood transfusions or doctors' appointments. Teddy would gaze around the waiting-room at the other patients and, thinking that he was so much more privileged than they, would feel sad on their behalf. One day he thanked a doctor for 'giving me courage'. 'No,' replied the doctor, 'I've helped you find your own.' He was sometimes in pain and nearly always discomfort, but he complained less than at any other time in his whole life. His reaction to his illness was in character: he was stoical, often funny, but completely resigned. Only the uncomplaining wasn't typical. A rota of care, meals and visits from friends was organised. Somehow his rest time had to be protected, but people who had come from India, America or Italy just to see him had to be allowed their visiting rights. One afternoon after a particularly social day he said, 'I'm going to leave quite a hole in my friends' lives when I go, aren't I?'

Every day he spoke about his plan to go back to Patmos. Few of us believed he would be strong enough for the journey. On the day that his stalwart carer, his niece and a temporary nurse got him on the plane to Athens, he was almost unconscious. But Teddy had surprising qualities for such a gentle person, and determination was one of them.

They took a helicopter from Athens which was met by Teddy's boat man. He put Teddy in a wheelchair, and pushed him through the narrow cobbled streets to the house. A bed had been put in the upper sitting-room where the windows overlooked the mountain of Profitis Ilias. On Teddy's fiftieth birthday we had climbed to the top with Bruce for a midnight picnic.

He wasn't able to open his eyes much, but whenever he heard a noise he recognised – such as the donkeys braying – he would slowly turn his head in that direction and his expression would become calm and happy. The same thing happened when he realised friends were there. Twenty-four hours after his arrival it was clear he was just fading away. The medication was stopped and Teddy himself seemed to have decided not to eat.

His niece sorted through Teddy's untidy, eclectic record collection – through the Supremes, the Stones and Puccini – and found Strauss's *Four Last Songs*. This was played until the evening, when his maid Petroula indicated that there should be no more music. Living on an island without sophisticated medical facilities, she was experienced with dying and knew how things should be. After the sun had set she mimed that we shouldn't talk; voices would prevent the soul from departing easily. A long trestle table draped with an Indian hanging was carried into the room and on it was placed a winding-sheet.

With a friend holding his hand Teddy died in the early morning, easily and without any pain or struggle.

The uncharacteristic dark city suit that had been chosen to bury him in was covered with roses, plumbago and bougainvillea from the garden, until only Teddy's face was showing, floating above the blooms.

At midday he was carried through the house to the funeral bier. It had stood in the dusty street all morning, draped in black velvet and looking somewhat incongruous as the donkeys and chickens pushed past it. The crowd followed the bearers to the Convent of Zoodochou Piyi, where a short service took place. It had always been a special place for Teddy; every year he had paid for repairs to the roof and often visited the two elderly nuns who lived there. We filed out past the body and everyone kissed or touched his forehead. And then we trailed through the town again till we reached the burial ground on the side of the hill overlooking Profitis Ilias and beyond it the sea. Cypress trees shaded the graves; at the head of each one was a plain cross on a plinth which contained a small niche with a glass door. Here were kept photographs of the dead person, family mementoes, a candle and sometimes a little snack in case the soul wandered off course and got hungry on its journey. The candle, helping to guide the soul, would be kept alight for forty days and Petroula had also left one burning in Teddy's bedroom.

We watched the heavy slabs being lifted and the body in its winding-sheet lowered into the shallow stone grave.

If Teddy had arranged his death and funeral himself, particular as he was, I don't think he would have done it differently.

CHAPTER 33

On Safari

In 1989, the same year that Bruce died, Candy decided to move with Kezzie and live with us in London. Although David had told Candy that his marriage was over and he no longer slept with his wife, when Kezzie was a year old and a new baby arrived it was obvious that this wasn't true and that he had no intention of leaving home.

Kezzie had once seen two boys at the local swimming pool, one a bit younger than her and one a bit older. 'I think they might be my brothers,' she said to me. A couple of years later, when she was living in London but on a visit to the Tower, she thought she spotted David across the street. I had left her in W. H. Smith's while I finished my shopping. She got bored with their pathetic selection of children's literature and went to sit on the pavement outside. A young friend was with her and he reported back to me that Kezzie had shouted across the street to a man outside Woolworth's, ''Ere! Is your name David? I think you're my dad.' Indeed, it was David and he came over and gave them some money for sweets.

Candy and Kezzie's move to London meant a lot of shuffling and re-arranging of rooms. I didn't want to move Tom, who had a large room incorporating a small kitchen at the top of the house. My room was on the same floor. It was smaller, but big enough for Kezzie and Candy. I bought a beautiful boat-shaped bed for me and installed it in the family room which led off the kitchen on the first floor. Marilyn had her work area at one end of the sitting-room on the ground floor. I put a sofa bed at the other end so that I could sleep there if the family room was being used for lunch or dinner parties. Candy, Kezzie and I were all a bit squashed, but as the arrangement was for our benefit, it seemed only fair that neither George nor Tom would have to squeeze up. It worked well: I was pleased that the family was all under one roof; Candy was pleased to have our support and more opportunities for finding a job; Kezzie was pleased to see so much of Uncle Tom whom she loved (and Tom was pleased for the same reason). George put up with anything that made me happy.

Now that Greckel was out of the picture (and no longer wishing to be part of the household), when George wasn't on tour he was home a lot more. The band was getting a huge amount of work and George could no longer be described as 'fat and fairly famous' – he was fat and famous.

That winter I decided that I could safely take off on my own and come back to a family intact. The Tower was let until March, Candy had found work and Kezzie was at nursery school. Tom's future was still uncertain: he had come back from a tour of the Middle East with Derek Nimmo's company, appearing as a guards officer in an old-fashioned play called *The Reluctant Debutante*. Since then no other parts had come his way and he was working, quite happily, in a second-hand bookshop in Notting Hill. Home in time to babysit.

I decided to go to Kenya and chose a safari which was quite low-budget and involved putting up one's own tent at the various stops. We started off from Nairobi and on the seven-hour bumpy drive to the Masai Mara I realised I hated the only other member of our party. And he hated me. Kenya had just begun to recover from a tourist slump, but not enough for the safari that I had so carefully chosen to attract more than two people: me and Phillip, an ill-matched pair. Phillip was a security guard and about forty years old. He had a slightly pointed head, a grey complexion and a very small symmetrical moustache. His face was usually set in an angry expression and his demeanour was cowed. He loved to grumble.

His only interest in going on safari seemed to be photographing animals mating; when we stopped at a market to buy provisions for our evening meal, he bought postcards of them doing it. His other ambition appeared to be to avoid sharing his cigarettes. As I had triumphantly given up smoking when Kezzie was two years old this didn't bother me, but our 'staff' were puzzled. There was Anthony our guide, David our cook and Jonathan our driver, all Christian and all devout smokers. They had assumed that Phillip, like all other 'rich' Westerners, would share.

This mutual hatred had an advantage. If I had been one of a homogeneous group I would have sat with them round the camp fire. As things turned out, Phillip sat grumpily on his own; I sat with the staff and heard about their lives. They called me Mama.

After the Masai Mara we camped at Saiwa swamp, the Kakamega forest, the lakes Victoria, Nakuru and Naivasha. Our final destination was to be Mount Elgon.

When we first arrived at our chosen spot one of the men would help me put up my tent. They didn't help Phillip.

In my tent I unrolled my length of foam and shook out my sleeping bag. I folded half my clothes into a pillow and slept in the other half. I used my hat as a bedside table and put my pills, my torch, my antihistamine cream and my clock inside the crown. Instead of Radio 4 to lull me to sleep there were the hippos grunting and the sound of David, Anthony and Jonathan talking quietly in soothing voices as they tidied the camp.

It became my job to erect the shower tent: a screen of sarongs ensured a degree of privacy, and hanging above this on a branch was a bucket of water. A rope was tied to the bucket's handle and when jerked the water came splashing down.

I usually helped David prepare our dinner (his speciality was banana fritters and custard). The hated Phillip joined us to eat but always sat a little apart. He never looked at anyone, but sat hunched up with his chin buried in his chest, his furtive piggy eyes darting from side to side but never engaging with anyone else.

Our last camp was at the foot of Mount Elgon, which bestrides the border of Kenya and Uganda. We had planned to visit the Elgon salt caves. In that area elephants have a shortage of salt in their diet, so they follow their leader into the caves in the evening and spend all night licking away at the salt. They come in such large herds that not only is it a spectacular sight but they are also at risk from poachers. I was half-way through peeling a yam for supper when we heard shots ring out. Poachers aren't fussy about how they get money, so Anthony didn't hesitate. 'Get your passports and wallets, extinguish your lamps, leave everything else and follow me quickly to the Land Rover.'

The nearest town was only an hour's drive and there Anthony found us rooms in what appeared to be a brothel. The bedrooms had no windows and opened on to a central courtyard. In the downstairs bar I had a drink and sat under a large portrait of Chairman Moi and opposite a painting, of a pretty Victorian Miss with two admirers, entitled *Two Strings to Her Bow*.

In spite of a mattress made of lumps, a cockroach the size of a mouse and the noise of the music and dancing from the bar, I slept well, glad to be away from the poachers and Mount Elgon, where it had been freezing and raining as well as dangerous.

After three weeks on the road I was looking forward to Lamu, an island 300 miles north of Mombasa, which was described in the guidebooks as having a 'languorous unspoilt atmosphere'. A small plane flew me and ten other passengers to the airstrip. Our luggage was unloaded on to a wheelbarrow and then on to a diesel launch which took us across the narrow strip of water to the island.

Lamu is an ancient, Arab trading town and the population is largely Muslim. The men wear full-length white robes and the women a liberalised version of the black wraparound bui bui.

I found a room overlooking the port where dhows were floating. Just out of sight was a donkey sanctuary. There were no cars. My room had two windows, a mirror, a mosquito net without holes and some hooks for my clothes. The owner said that if I had a 'special beach boy' I could take him to my room. I disappointed him on that, and tried to compensate by showing him all my family snaps.

Every morning I went to the post office in the hope of receiving a fax from home. I was getting very homesick. In spite of crab for supper, mangoes for breakfast, golden sand, warm sea, dhow rides and the friendship of two gay women I'd met, I wanted my family.

Tom wrote that George had written a long fax which had not gone through, as instead of the international code he had just added the telephone number and the fax one together. He went on to say that everyone was well, although Kezzie was crying because she had just dropped her toast in the bath.

Candy wrote to tell me how much she and Kezzie missed me and she wished Tom would cut his hair. She added a PS: 'You'll be pleased to hear that Greckel is getting married. George seems very relieved.'

George wrote, rather boringly, about the weather in London, and then added, 'There's been no squawk from the Greckel.' He signed his fax 'Captain Lobotomy' and I wondered what domestic disaster he had engineered to deserve his nickname. I would soon find out – in three days I was home.

CHAPTER 34

No Excellent Thing

Captain Lobotomy had earned his nickname after a train journey. He gave a lunchtime lecture in Bristol and afterwards, instead of getting on the train returning to London, he had landed up in Penzance. 'I had a lovely sleep,' he said defiantly, when he finally got back too late to eat the dinner that Candy and Tom had cooked for him.

His increasing deafness made his travelling life difficult. There was no way that he could hear the information that was broadcast through the station's loud-speakers. Also his eyesight was less than perfect and he couldn't read the information boards. If he asked for help from a member of the railway staff he couldn't hear the answer, especially if it was delivered in a rapid foreign accent.

Passing strangers could also be caught unawares by George's failing faculties. Having unwisely eaten a rather stale hot dog in Liverpool Street station he badly needed the lavatory. When his 20p piece refused to open the door he accosted a man in a white suit and clutching his stomach, demanded entry. The man failed to see any humour in being mistaken for a lavatory attendant and threatened to knock his fucking hat off.

But usually George was well known and often enough recognised to survive. He was working harder than ever. 1991 was a good year for the band, and his agent, Jack Higgins, was beginning to promote his art lectures successfully. Even August was busy that year, and as September was a good fishing month, we decided that he would take a week off and come down to the Tower with me. We planned to come back at the end of the month for Kezzie's fifth birthday. George had offered to pay for a Punch and Judy show for her, an event that he was looking forward to as much as Kezzie was.

The sitting-room, which now doubled as my bedroom, was above George's rooms and the night before we were due to leave for Wales I heard his phone ringing incessantly. I went down the next morning knowing it had to have been Greckel. Her marriage had only lasted a couple of months, and once or twice I had suspected that she was back on the trail.

George was sitting slumped in an armchair, his face was pale grey. He looked very old and sad. 'I can't come with you,' he said. 'She says she'll kill herself if I do.'

I sat in his uncomfortable 1930s armchair drinking tea, pretending to be reasonable.

Perhaps because George was exhausted it wasn't hard to persuade him to come with me. He made a phone call, established that she was not alone, and then we set off. He also told Greckel that before he came back to London he would finally make a decision as to whether he would stay with me or leave to be with her.

On the long drive down to the Tower I was astonished to learn how much he had been seeing her. Astonished because he had been able to make elaborate plans, arrange secret meetings, take her away on gigs, give her a weekly sum of money and neither Marilyn nor I had suspected anything. He had told me that he no longer saw her and I had believed him. And I wouldn't have thought it possible that he could hold such complicated arrangements in his head.

We stopped at the new supermarket in Abergavenny to buy groceries. I had a Dutch family arriving for bed and breakfast the following day. George stayed in the car and I wandered round the shop with my trolley trying to remember if it was the Dutch who only ate cheese and ham for breakfast.

I knew that I didn't want George to leave, but I wasn't quite sure why not. I also knew that George felt needed by Greckel and that I was not the neurotic child that he had once loved. Greckel's weakness was her strength. She had others: she was outrageous and funny – I knew that from her letters (which I always made a point of reading); she was sexually generous – in one of her letters she described giving someone 'dickie' because it was his birthday – and her letters were full of clothes being ripped, and behaviour that might well frighten the horses; she was also good at making George feel good – the letters were usually signed LYTB (love you to bits) and often mentioned the hardness of what she called 'your bits'.

I didn't want to compete – nor could I have done. I

wanted George to stay because he wanted to and not because of what I could talk him into. I wanted him to stay because we had been together for thirty years, because I cared for him, because of Kezzie, because of the Tower. I didn't want to make false promises to him. I didn't think I could change much, any more than he could, but I did say that if he decided to stay with me I wouldn't put up with any more Greckel or his duplicity. My priorities were now the family (including the cats) and my friends. George was part of that family. We were important to him too, but so were other things: his singing, his writing, his art collection, being recognised, his sexual freedom, and Greckel.

We didn't talk that week about how we would divide up the spoils if we separated, and I didn't say that I thought he'd be dead in a year if he went off with Greckel.

George fished and slept a lot and I fed the Dutch family their cheese and ham. They decided to stay until the end of the week and their presence lent a degree of normality to my day. I got out maps and guidebooks, told them which pubs would welcome children and how to use my washing machine.

The day came when he had to ring Greckel. 'I've decided to stay,' he said and I just nodded. There was a large window in the kitchen in front of which was a day bed. George sat there for what seemed like a long time, staring down at the oxbow and the willow that we'd planted for his fiftieth birthday. He picked up the phone. 'Stay there,' he said. 'I want you to hear what I say.' And he dialled. But at that moment the Dutch family came in, all smiles and compliments and asking for a jug of milk for their tea.

After they'd gone he rang Greckel and just said that he'd thought about it all week and that he had decided to stay with me.

That night we went to a party in the next village given by some neighbours. We didn't know them well, but we didn't want to be alone together and we needed not the kindness, but the distraction of strangers. We had nothing more to say to each other. I didn't feel triumphant, just fed up, cold and exhausted. George said he wouldn't ever see her again and that she always drew a line through people once an affair was over.

'Good,' I said. 'We won't go through that again.'

'It really is over this time. She says that she wants to get a new boyfriend and will I give her some money to get her teeth fixed.'

'Fine,' I replied, 'whatever,' and I stomped off to bed.

On my bedside table was my answerphone blinking away and showing that I had six messages.

The first one was from Pandora, the long-lost daughter. Her relationship with George hadn't quite ended, he was still paying for her analyst and meeting her once a week, and giving her money from time to time. But it wasn't money she needed, it was a father. She was now thirty, and she wanted a room in our house. Tom and Candy still lived with us, why couldn't she? George had used me as the reason why not. It was true that I would have hated it, also true that in spite of her offering to sleep in the kitchen, there wasn't a spare space, let alone a spare room; but, more importantly, George didn't want it. He didn't get on with her and that made him feel guilty.

The next five calls were from Greckel. Every time she rang she had to listen to my voice politely informing the caller about my bed and breakfast availability.

Greckel's voice was definitely no excellent thing: it was an affected, Bohemian whine. While making the calls she progressed to sounding drunk and then very drunk, and from insulting to threatening. I didn't like being called 'a boring nasty woman', a 'power maniac' who could make my husband do anything. She advised me to write another boring book and to stop preventing George from seeing Pandora. After the first call, which had begun with a long drawn-out 'Hi', the next four calls began with 'Hi – it's ME again.' The fourth call started with a description of cutting my head off and then described slicing me up into pieces, putting me on skewers and roasting me. In the fifth and last call she accused me of having 'no fucking guts'.

I sat on the bed listening for the sound of a car careering drunkenly down the drive. The weather was matching Greckel's rage. Autumn gales were gusting round the Tower, rattling the windows and adding to my fear. It wasn't that I thought that she would really break in wielding an axe, but her voice, even more than her words, had sounded full of sinister intent, and I fully expected a brick through the window.

Thankfully the Dutch family had gone, so the next morning we were able to leave early for London. I hadn't slept much and was feeling very fragile, certainly in no mood for a birthday party with a Punch and Judy show. I played the tape again the next morning. It hadn't got any better, and I played it to George, who said, 'She was drunk. She won't do you any harm.'

We stopped at my favourite pub on the way back. I sat there crying, not caring about the curious stares of the other customers. She has *done* me harm, I thought. I do feel damaged.

CHAPTER 35

Let's Try Abroad

I was grateful for the party and the Punch and Judy show. We had to behave well and no one noticed the state of shock that George and I were in.

When the children had gone I played the tape to Anna Coote, one of my great friends. We had met when she was pregnant with Ruby, who was born a few months before Kezzie. Ruby, small, blonde and friendly, and Kezzie, tall, dark and 'confrontational', had also become close friends. Every summer the four of us went on holiday together, once camping in France, but usually going to Patmos, the island where Teddy lived. Being a grandmother I didn't have friends with children the same age as Kezzie, but Anna was only ten years younger than me and it was a close and easy relationship. Anna was not only a sympathetic friend, she was also a formidable woman. Her many books included *Sweet Freedom*, which she wrote with Bea Campbell about the feminist movement, the self-explanatory *Guide to Women's Rights* and *Power and Prejudice*. At the time of Kezzie's party she was the deputy director of the left-wing think tank, IPPR. My wise and wonderful friend, having listened in an amazed silence to the tape, suggested I send it to my solicitor. 'Just in case,' she said, 'and tell Greckel what you've done.' She suggested this because she thought I might need that kind of evidence if there was a divorce. I had a different reason. I was frightened, perhaps because I'd just seen the film *Fatal Attraction*.

The next morning I left the house early to go to a press showing of a film. Tom came with me and we sat together on the bus in a careful silence. I didn't want to involve him in what might seem like a loyalty contest.

When I got home there was a letter from George. He wrote that he'd gone to see Greckel to give her the money she needed to get her teeth fixed. 'Don't think I'll be turned round,' he continued. 'I'm quite determined this time.'

A few days later a letter to George from Greckel arrived. She was distraught, angry, and sad. She said that she had paid a lot of money to a lawyer to stop the story getting into the papers; that she had only been dumped because she'd lost her driving licence; that some of her friends had wanted to do George some physical damage; and she reminded him that he had promised to put a bit of money into her bank account each month. There were pages of accusations, but every other paragraph expressed her sorrow that the relationship had ended.

And for two years it seemed as if it had.

GEORGE HAD A major health scare in 1993. In the lavatory of the Colchester Playhouse where he was going to sing, George haemorrhaged and thought he was going to follow his father who had died in his sixties of a stomach ulcer. Instead, he hauled himself along an empty corridor on his hands and knees, summoned help and was raced to the hospital in an ambulance.

A few days later there was a large photograph in the local paper over the heading, 'George's laughter tonic.' The text read 'Chirpy jazzman George Melly showed he was well on the way to recovery as he cracked jokes from his hospital bed. The nurses praised Mr Melly as a "brilliant patient".' Presumably they hadn't heard the jokes before.

That Christmas he did Ronnie Scott's as usual, but as he was tired, and also fretful because the doctors had told him to stop smoking, I booked us a holiday in Egypt. We flew everywhere. George only had a few days between two jobs, and therefore we could only be away for six days. George is not a good traveller. He complains a lot: babies crying, putting his seat in the upright position, filling in non-resident forms. We had one altercation before we landed in Cairo when we were told to put our watches on by two hours, 'to 11.40'. George heard 'to 11.14.' I pointed out that not only were my ears in better working order, but if he was right it would mean the time difference was 1 hour and 34 minutes which seemed improbable. George could not grasp the logic of this.

I dragged him round the Valley of the Kings, but the temple at Karnak, overwhelming in its proportions, over-whelmed George and he retired to our hotel, once a palace of King Farouk. He fared a little better in Aswan. Most of the important sights – the temples of Philae, Kalabusha and the Mausoleum of the Aga Khan – could be gazed at while lying back in a felucca.

Cairo was less successful. He bravely mounted a camel for the obligatory ride, and even looks quite jolly in the photograph, but the pyramid of Cheops was a bad idea. I had failed to read the warning in the guidebook, that 'crawling through the narrow passageway that led to the pharaoh's chamber was not for the claustrophobic or faint-hearted'. George wasn't either of those things, but in order not to bang one's head on the roof of the tunnel it was necessary to proceed in a crouched position. He hated it and said the Pyramids were just what he expected, big and pointed. It was our last day and by the time we reached the airport George had finished off his bottle of whisky.

He had also completely ignored my dietary advice – taken from the guidebook – and the whisky, the large quantities of meat and unwashed fruit now combined to create havoc with his bowels and he spent the entire flight home in the lavatory.

'I think I'd prefer a fishing holiday,' he said.

When I was in Kenya in 1992 I had read about big-game fishing off the coast near Mombasa, so when, three years later, the *Evening Standard* asked George if he would do a holiday piece, I thought we might be able to enjoy the few things we had in common. He loved the idea of looking at animals on safari, and although he didn't think sea fishing would be a patch on catching trout, he was willing to try. I liked the animals too – and also sleeping in a tent.

I decided that we would take Kezzie with us. The *Standard* was only paying for George, but as we would all share a room or a tent the cost would be affordable. Kezzie was eight years old and liked reading, so I knew that the long airport waits would be bearable for her. Candy was away a lot doing a degree course in child development and although Tom was still living at home he had a job and often spent the night at his girlfriend's. So either Kezzie came with us or I stayed at home with her. That would have meant George staying at home too. Getting around in Britain could cause him problems, but they were minor ones; once he entered an airport terminal he was a lost soul.

We had an idyllic time. Kezzie made friends with a mongoose and two waiters called Abel and Joseph, George caught some huge fish and fell in love with Africa, I learnt to snorkel and tried to keep my party in order. One of the entries in Kezzie's diary reads, 'George slipped in the water and cut his knee. And when I gave him the book he was in the water and dropped the book and got it soaking. And me and George got into trouble by granny.'

Much as I had loved our holiday, when the *Evening Standard* suggested another one, fishing for salmon in Russia, I decided it wasn't quite my thing. I knew there would be mosquitoes the size of horse flies and the weather would be freezing. Tom volunteered to do the minding. I soaked their clothes and mosquito nets in a liquid that was supposed to deter the insects and bought them outfits that covered their faces with a fine net.

When they arrived at their camp on the Kola river south of Murmansk, the weather had taken a turn for the worse. Although it was summer the tundra was frozen, a gale blew round their tent and even the mosquitoes stayed away. During the day George and Tom lay in their sleeping bags reading the *Gormenghast* trilogy and drinking vodka. At night they raced across to the dining tent to join the other foolhardy fishermen, drank more vodka and had salmon for dinner: either curried, fried, baked, turned into fish cakes, kedgeree or rock-hard pizzas.

The following winter the *Standard* suggested South Africa and Kezzie, George and I set off for Cape Town. Our first stop was a bleak, deserted holiday camp on the southern-most tip of the continent. We were meant to meet some people who would take George out shark-fishing, but they never showed up. Once we had stood on a rock and marvelled at the fact that there was nothing between us and the South Pole, we ran out of entertainments. Swimming was out of the question as a wind, known as 'the Cape doctor', blew the sand around like mini sand-storms. We drove back to Cape Town. Kezzie had run out of books by this time and she and George were quarrelling about who should sit in the front. Kezzie thought she should because she was – or said she was – car-sick in the back, and George thought he should because of age and seniority. Kezzie won, partly because we half believed the car-sick story and partly because I didn't want George in the front talking non-stop. I was in quite a bad temper.

We 'did' Cape Town in a half-hearted sort of way. The high spot for Kezzie was meeting Venetia who was visiting friends there. George, who complained about Venetia as often as she complained about him, was not averse to repeating his complaints over dinner and for some reason Kezzie loved it. 'Any Venetia stories?' she would demand and usually George would oblige. Also Venetia now had a title, which seemed to impress Kezzie.

Our last stop was a very grand game reserve near Port Elizabeth. It had four-poster beds, private balconies and boasted 'the atmosphere of an Edwardian country manor'. Our brochure informed us that we were 'contributing to conserving a vanishing way of life'. Every evening we sat in the vast dining-room surrounded by photographs of elephants. Finding a suitable subject of conversation was hard. One night when Kezzie was describing the life cycle of the tomato plant at the same time as George was listing the faults of Salvadore Dali's wife I went to the lavatory to count up to ten. When I came back George was regaling Kezzie with dirty jokes. At least they looked happy, but next year, I thought, we'll go back to Kenya.

CHAPTER 36

Not Really a Castle

George became even more famous during the 1990s. When I gave my name on the telephone, the response was often 'Any relation?' I usually replied, 'Only by marriage' as if I was married to some cousin several times removed. But George has never had any problems with being famous and the consequent publicity; he enjoys it and happily agrees to exposure that some more reticent people might find intrusive.

Anthony Clare has interviewed him for his series on the Seven Ages of Man and George has three times been the subject of *Through the Keyhole*, a television programme where the owner's house is invaded by cameras and Loyd Grossman. What they film is then shown to a panel, hosted by David Frost, who encourages the team members to guess the identity of the home owner from various clues; in George's case, books on Surrealism, fishing-rods and many images of headless ladies. He has happily and enthusiastically talked about his homosexuality, his libido and eventual lack of it, his marriage, his morals and his atheism on various TV shows and in newspaper articles:

'In Bed with George Melly'
'Things Run Smoothly Since I Lost my Libido'
'A Man Who Never Said No to Almost Anything'
'A Triumph of Excess'
'Sex, Art and the Glory of George'.

A journalist who interviewed him for a Sunday paper described his 'formidable pursuit of sex and drink', and me, quite incorrectly, as 'his long-suffering wife'.

Anything goes, well almost. He did refuse to appear on the Graham Norton show. They had asked him to have a plaster cast made of his erect penis which would then be discussed by Graham and the audience. The researcher explained that the sculptor was willing to do anything within reason that would facilitate a flattering size. Apparently even George draws the line somewhere.

No one has ever said an unkind word about him – in print. Family and work colleagues, whether they are secretaries, agents or band members, are another matter.

Sometimes it's irritating always to be greeted at a party with 'Hello, Diana, where's George?' And the musicians don't always like it when their skilful solos are not applauded with quite the same enthusiasm as George's singing. George needs to be centre-stage. He would not be the success he is if that were not the case. For ten years I was his biggest fan, and then I began to struggle away from him. It was hard for him too, and the more I pushed him away the more he tried to regain his place as the centre of my life. I was the one at the end of the row who wasn't clapping. He tried hard, but I sat with my hands tucked under my bottom. At least my growing independence gave him a freedom that a more doting wife would not have allowed him.

There weren't many times when I minded that George got all the credit for things that I had done, but I did mind about the Tower: it was my project, my success and I was jealous of it. I had found it, made it beautiful and turned it into a successful business.

The clients who rented the house and fishing returned every year and the Welsh Tourist Board kept me busy with bed and breakfast clients. Alison Lurie, the American writer, had written about me and the house in an article called 'The Benevolent Tower' and I was able to use it for publicity.

About three times a year a party of five fishermen would arrive. Memories of my wet fishing honeymoon in Scotland were useful – I knew the score. The men had early-morning tea and then went down to the river. They would come back for breakfast and I would cook them their trout, and just like boiled eggs, some liked them well-done and some under-done. While they sat over their coffee I made them piles of sandwiches and home-made soup in a Thermos. They always brought nice wine with them and dinner was a pleasure. I usually cooked a stew or a curry so that the meal could be advanced if the fish weren't biting or delayed if they were. An advantage of their numbers was that they could bore each other with fishing tales, unlike George, who usually fished alone and could only bore me. Jeremy Paxman came a couple of times and on one occasion I explained that there were too many of them and he would have to sleep in a tent. Tom was there and took great pleasure in fixing up the tent with a little bedside table, a Calor gas light and a camp bed. Paxman looked with horror at his sleeping arrangements and said that he'd thought I'd been joking. 'Kate Adie wouldn't have made such a fuss,' replied Tom.

It was inevitable that people would congratulate George on the wonderful Tower, and it always annoyed me. TV companies were the worst offenders. The first company to arrive were making a programme called *Great Growers* about celebrities and their gardens. It didn't worry them that George's knowledge of our garden was restricted to where I allowed him to dig for worms.

Apart from the cameraman, his assistant and three electricians, there was Alice the producer and Mary the presenter, a woman of about forty, attractive, tall, with black hair and freckles, and wearing unsuitable high-heeled boots.

'Would you all like coffee?' I said.

'Brilliant,' replied Alice. 'Now, George, we'd like to do the first shot with you lying under the catalpa tree and talking about how you found this brilliant castle.'

George looked anxious, he hadn't a clue what a catalpa tree was. 'Well, it's not really a castle, and it was actually Diana who found it and planted the garden. Wouldn't we have her in this shot?'

Alice looked round at me and I said hopefully, 'I could change out of these clothes and put some lipstick on.'

But Alice knew what she wanted, and it wasn't me. 'Oh, don't worry, dear, the asparagus bed is in the next shot and we can have you in the background brandishing a hoe or something. OK, Mary, we're ready to go.'

Mary licked her lips and smiled at the camera. 'This is Mary Dawson. Welcome to *Great Growers*. I'm with George Melly the well-known singer and raconteur in his fabulous garden in Wales. George . . .'

But George missed his cue. As Mary announced herself, he suddenly remembered that years ago they had had an affair lasting some weeks. After they'd gone, we sat round the table having a cup of tea. Our conversation went like this:

George: Did you know who she was?

Diana: How could I? I've never even met her. Like you, I only clicked when I heard her name.

George: I thought she was rather spiky, didn't you?

Diana: Well, I'd be spiky if someone I'd been to bed with didn't recognise me.

George: Well, how do we know she recognised me?

Diana: Don't be silly, she knew it was going to be you.

George: What?

Diana: Nothing.

George: Actually, I can't remember much about her, how it ended or anything.

Diana: I can.

George: Oh, did we just get bored?

Diana: No, you gave her the clap.

That wasn't the only time a starring role was denied me. A couple of years later another TV company decided to make a film about our famous local restaurateur and George. They asked if I would be in it and, although professing indifference, I was flattered.

The chef was to be fishing with George, who would then

help him cook in my kitchen. I was to join them for lunch. They were going to cook pasta as it was unlikely they would catch fish on a cold wet March day.

This was a typically daft TV idea as George can't cook and the chef couldn't fish.

I spent the evening choosing clothes that didn't look as if I cared, and then washed my hair.

At six o'clock the next morning they all arrived. It was pouring with rain and they didn't have any gumboots for the river shoot. One of them was frightened of cows. Quite right, I told her, they're much nastier than the bull. Rather impressively I found them ten pairs of gumboots – all the sizes were written inside in black ink.

George seemed to be calling the director 'Cuddles', but whether that *was* her name, or because she was buxomly built and wearing lots of levels of skirt and T-shirt (managing none the less to show bits of bosom, bottom and thigh), I didn't know.

While they were at the river the producer asked me if I could remember any 'amusing' stories about the restaurant. I dredged up one about eating there with Edna O'Brien in the mid-1960s. I felt slightly embarrassed about name-dropping, but as the director hadn't heard of Edna I needn't have worried. The punch-line fell rather flat and she continued to look expectantly at me.

When they came back from the river, Cuddles was screaming with laughter at George's jokes and the producer set the table for lunch: two places only. 'We thought we'd just have the boys together,' she said.

I didn't really *mind* about being rejected, but as the room was now choc-à-bloc with sound and lighting men I felt very anxious about getting any of the pasta. Cuddles was on her mobile and the producer on *my* phone. She hadn't asked.

I retired to the garden and was hacking at an overgrown elderflower bush when the lovely chef appeared with a plate of steaming pasta, a glass of Chardonnay and a sweet smile. The sun had come out, they'd soon be gone, I thought, and I'd make George put all the furniture back.

CHAPTER 37

Tippex and Revenge

Two years passed before George started seeing Greckel again. At first there were some angry phone calls, and once she sent him an envelope with just a paying-in slip inside to indicate that she wanted money. But the peace didn't last. To begin with he didn't see her very often, but by 1999 it was obvious that he was going to resume some kind of relationship with her and I felt angry and hurt. When he decided to stay with me he'd promised never to see her again, but I should have known that people don't – or can't – keep those sorts of promises. At least it was agreed that there would be no secrecy, and so their dates were recorded in the diary.

When I saw 'lunch, Greck, Soho' written in, my heart would thump and I would feel frightened and sick. George knew this and he wished I didn't. So, as he also minded the row and my subsequent coldness, he sometimes saw no need to mention their arrangements. Somehow I always knew, or if not always, often. Her aura was so powerful and threatening for me that I could almost smell her when they were in contact.

I hated being in the house and involved with some dreary domestic task when he made his jaunty exit and then came back from one of their dates, all dressed up in one of his stripy suits, light-hearted and a bit tipsy.

Eventually I found ways to cope with my rage. Once I invited some friends for lunch on a day when 'Greck 1 o'clock. Soho' was in the diary. He came through the dining-room, saw the table rather beautifully set and said, 'Ah, a lunch party?' 'Yes,' I said. 'Little Nell and James Fox.' And just for a moment his face lost its cheerful smile. But revenge isn't all that sweet, and I usually felt too depressed to organise anything so ambitious. Once I just let him think I'd left him. Kezzie was away on a school trip. I double-locked the front door so that when he returned home he assumed the house must be empty. I stayed in my room for two days, just creeping out to get something to eat and make a solitary visit to the cinema. His deafness made this rather pointless fiction easy to maintain, and as I was calmer by the time I showed myself, perhaps it was better than making a scene.

The only revenge that was any fun involved Tippex. 'Lunch Greck' was written in for a date two weeks off. I Tippexed it out. I didn't do it very carefully, and the Tippex made bumpy, ragged little mountains on the page in his diary. I was sure that he would notice, that he would remember his date or that she would remind him and I would be found out. His sister, Andrée, who was staying with us, also dreaded Greckel, which made the situation more enjoyable, particularly when I saw that with some difficulty George had scratched a new lunch date over the bumpy Tippex, this time with a different ex-girlfriend. On the morning of the lunch Andrée was in his room while he was getting dressed and was able to report that Greckel had rung up and was not only outraged not to be given lunch but furious that he hadn't even bothered to write it in his diary. George told Andrée that he was terrified that he would bump into Greckel somewhere in Soho and she would see that his story of a business lunch was not true.

Some days later I told him what I'd done. It took some time to explain, as he didn't know what Tippex was, and I had to get some to demonstrate. But then he laughed and said it was very funny and that the band would think so too. I wonder if he told her and if she thought it was funny; she's meant to be 'such a scream'. I don't think I could stretch my sense of humour that far.

I gave up on revenge, and sometimes I think I've given up minding. For my own sake I know I should. And I even try to be pleased that he's seeing someone who cheers him up, but I'm a long way off achieving that noble goal.

CHAPTER 38

The Support Team

Our marriage, like many, has been quite a power struggle. When we were first together I controlled George with my needs, my childishness and my neurosis. It was unconscious control, but successful. I have replaced it with a different kind. I am like the possessive secretary with the successful boss. Not for nothing am I called the Wing Co. (Our company is called Wing Commander Jack Ltd and Jack is a nodding reference to George's sojourn in the Navy.) But I am good at my job. I manage the money, the diary, the medication and mediate between Shirley, who has been our secretary since Marilyn left, and Jack, George's agent. They don't get on. Shirley is only with us for two half-days a week, but, knowing nothing of George's world of journalism, art and jazz, she finds that side of things perplexing and is sometimes still quarrelling with Jack or shouting at her computer until after six. Also she has no idea of the geography of England: Newcastle and Plymouth could as well be next door to each other, so plotting a journey for

George to sing in different towns is almost impossible. Politically we inhabit different planets. George once heard her saying to an Indian man who was collecting for an Asian charity, 'This is a Christian household.' And once she told me that she is careful what she says in front of George as she knows he is Jewish.

In spite of these drawbacks, I like her very much. She is very patient with George and doesn't automatically tell him when he is repeating a joke to her. Her looks and figure are motherly but she has long beautiful legs which George appreciates. She loves animals and will hold Bobby and Joey for me when I'm forcing worm pills down their little throats. Perhaps, more importantly, she is reliable, never ill and allows me to think I'm the boss.

Jack, five years older than George and into his eighties, has always looked after himself and likes to point out how much fitter and healthier he is than *some* of his clients. He has no time for the aches and pains of old age. I like him and I like the way he relies on me to know what's going on. He can ring me up on my mobile when I'm out walking and I can tell him, more or less accurately, what's in George's diary. We also discuss recipes, cats and the difficulty of contacting George when he's not at home. Jack is always demanding to know why I don't get George a mobile phone. Endlessly I explain that the ringing tone is too silent, and the instructions beyond him. I thought the problem could be solved with a pager. This small machine would simply vibrate, alerting its owner to ring a designated number – me or Jack. When a couple of weeks passed without George ever responding to it, I asked him to put it in his pocket so that we could test it. Twice I dialled its number but each time George rang me back to say that it didn't vibrate. Eventually we discovered the reason: George was carrying round an electric razor.

Once a month we have a book-keeper who comes in to sort out the papers for the accountant and do the dreaded VAT. Lyn is a single parent with two daughters. She has lovely red hair and twelve guinea pigs. One of them, Danny, used to be Kezzie's, but Kezzie gave him to me. 'Would you like him to be your very own?' she once said. 'After all, you are the one who cleans out his cage and feeds him.' My excuse for handing Danny on to Lyn was that he was lonely. He once had a companion, a rabbit called Eggs, but Eggs turned against Danny and so our cleaner, Alexandra, took him/her off our hands. Danny really was lonely and had a much better home with Lyn. Either Lyn or the other guinea pigs taught him to do guinea-pig speak. Apparently they have twenty-two different sounds.

Although Kezzie isn't exactly part of my support team she is an important member of the house. Aged eleven she started secondary school in West London. Candy had moved to South London to live with her partner, Mark, and as we had also moved from Ladbroke Grove to Shepherd's Bush, which was reasonably near the school, Kezzie began to live with us permanently. It was a bigger change for her than I realised. Although she had always lived half the time with us it *was* only half the time. Now with Candy the other side of London it meant that she would only see her at weekends. With all these changes being forced upon her, Kezzie decided to change something for herself. She had been christened Katherine and was known as Katie, she now let it be known that her name was 'Keziah', Kezzie for short. Within a few months, the name Katie was forgotten.

I have been a good grandmother to Kezzie. I found it much easier than being a mother. There are fewer parties and no unsuitable lovers to distract me. When I tell Kezzie that I am quite happy listening to Radio 4 and cleaning out a cupboard, she says, 'Why don't you get a life', but I have a life and I like it.

We have also moved from Wales to Berkshire. The Tower was not a suitable place for two elderly people. It was isolated, a long way from the station, the stone steps (both inside and out) would not be good for arthritic knees and, most important, the fishing was hard work. It was quite a long walk across the fields and the Usk is a spate river. When George wasn't back until after dark I used to become anxious.

Through friends I found a cottage that had once belonged to the actor Michael Hordern, a keen fisherman. It was four miles from the station and four minutes from the pub. The fishing was on easy water nearby. Although there was no local shop there were good neighbours and the Water Mill Theatre, just opposite, gave the village a lively atmosphere. At the back of the house was a long brick shed that once housed a large bread oven. When converted, this building would make a perfect room for Kezzie, now a teenager who needed space. There was plenty of room for other grandchildren too.

Tom had split up with the girlfriend he once had and married her successor. Lu was very popular with all of us and in 1998 their son Django was born – in a water bath in their front living-room. Tom's computer was housed in the same room: their lodger had a camera and the photographs of the birth (one of them has Tom in the bath with Lu) were quickly scanned and I saw my grandson's crumpled face and very long body within minutes of his arrival.

Our large garden in Bagnor has fruit trees and old-fashioned roses. At the back is a gate that opens on to a sloping field behind which are woods. Perfect for a dog, I thought.

Almost my last B&B guests at the Tower had been a couple who were farmers from Norfolk. The woman, Sally, was born profoundly deaf because her mother had contracted German measles when pregnant. She told me that her life had changed when she got a 'hearing dog'. Her dog, Blossom, not only made her feel safe in their farmhouse when her husband was away, but it alerted her to the telephone, the doorbell, the fire alarm and any other noise that she needed to hear. I decided that George would qualify for one, and it would be a welcome addition to the Support Team.

CHAPTER 39

. . . as a Post

A few months ago we were eating in a restaurant where some soft, rather boring piano music was being played. Soft it was, but not soft enough. George tried talking through it and although I could hear him, in no way could he hear any reply of mine. I scribbled him a note on the back of the menu: 'As you can't hear me, let's just not speak until the piano player has his break.' George scribbled back, 'Why don't I talk and you just nod?' 'I'm not the nodding kind,' I scribbled back.

On our honeymoon, which was when I realised he was a little deaf, I also discovered that not only did he not drive, he couldn't map-read either. When we should have been within a few miles of our destination in the north of Scotland, I saw a sign saying 'Carlisle [which is on the English border] 5 miles'. We had driven for two hours in the wrong direction and we had our first row. In the ensuing frost I switched on the radio, and there was George, discussing the charms of Greta Garbo on *Woman's Hour*. We listened in silence.

It's possible that deafness, unlike some disabilities, is

harder on the family than on the person. Certainly for George, who had always preferred talking and telling jokes and stories to listening, being deaf didn't seem to worry him. He enjoyed repeating his more absurd mis-hearings. Friends didn't mind either. George's good humour seemed to quell any irritation that they might feel on having endlessly to repeat themselves. But the same could not be said for me and I became very impatient with his failure to hear the telephone, the doorbell or anything faintly interesting that I might want to say. Eventually I found conversation with him so difficult that I stopped making any effort to chat or tell him things. Some nights we sit opposite each other in an uncomfortable silence. This is because George has forgotten his hearing-aid. He can't quite be bothered to go and look for it, and I'm fed up with crawling on my hands and knees under his bed in search. George is very uncomfortable with the silence so he hums a little, tries a question: 'Did you have a nice day?' But as I refuse to shout over my kedgeree he can't hear the answer.

Sometimes he is deafer than at other times, and if I have spent an evening shouting out my news, I find that the association of shouting and temper is enough to put me in a bad mood. Occasionally Kezzie will ask me why I'm cross with George and I tell her that I'm not, my voice at a certain pitch just *sounds* angry.

It took a lot of persuasion to convince George that a hearing dog would solve some of the problems, but finally he accepted the idea. We were on the waiting list for a year. During that time our Shepherd's Bush house and the cottage, as well as our family set-up and George's complicated life, were carefully vetted by the Hearing Dog

Association. The dog had to be large enough not to get squashed on railway-station platforms, but not so large that it would take up too much room in a car. It would also have to ride in the basket of his mobility bike when he went to the river. The dog would go to all George's gigs and mustn't bark at the wrong moment.

All hearing dogs are cat-friendly and apparently will urinate and defecate on command. They are trained to respond to your own telephone and doorbell, they will then alert you by pawing or nudging, and lead you to the source of the sound. If it's an emergency, the dog would just lie in the dead position at the recipient's feet. This could be a life-saver: George once set the smoke alarm off with the kettle steam and stood underneath the wailing sound, completely oblivious, while the rest of the house came running.

In London the garden was considered safe, but at the cottage it was necessary to have it fenced in. When we had passed all the tests we went to meet Max, our chosen dog, a Lhasa Apso. But George was becoming nervous at the responsibility that he was beginning to realise would be all his: he had to be the one man in Max's life, he had to walk him, feed him and love him. Until they had really 'bonded' Kezzie and I would not get a look in.

The next stage of their bonding would entail George's going to the Hearing Dog Centre to stay in a cottage with Max for a week. Jack was told (much to his irritation) that he mustn't book George for that period. Kezzie was delighted to hear that she would get a day off school to go to visit them. I went to Pets R Us and bought bowls and brushes. And then George changed his mind.

CHAPTER 40

In Sickness and in Health

One weekend in 2000 Django was staying with me. We were playing toddler games (something I've always hated), when I heard a loud thump coming from George's sitting-room. He had fainted but seemed none the worse for it and said that he had just fallen asleep while sitting at his desk and lost his balance on waking.

Django was an early riser and I was awake and making his breakfast when George buzzed down on his intercom at six o'clock, asking me to come up.

He was in bed looking very shaky and there was a trail of blood leading from his shower room. He said that he had fainted or fallen several more times in the night and cut his forehead.

I had always worried that George's choice of bedroom on the second floor was going to present problems. Had he been on the first floor I would have heard the thump, or if we'd had the dog he would have known to come and get me

– Max was going to be trained to fetch me if something bad happened to George.

Although it was a weekend and our GP's surgery was closed, their emergency service responded by sending round a locum who took a history and called an ambulance. Leaving Kezzie lying on the sofa suffering with a severe stomach ache, Django and I climbed into the ambulance with George and set off for the hospital. As we sped along the Westway, Django speechless with excitement, George removed his oxygen mask and said, 'I can't face having a hearing dog.'

I knew I couldn't argue, but I realised how much I had been looking forward to having a dog again, and how disappointed Kezzie was going to be.

George was in hospital for a week and had to cancel a fishing trip to Canada where the BBC wanted to send him to describe catching salmon. He was diagnosed with heart failure and COPD. Depending on your point of view, it was a good thing that George's selective hearing enabled him to deny that he had either of these ailments – heart failure he denied because it sounds worse than it is, and COPD (chronic obstructive pulmonary disease) because it meant ending a life-long love affair with cigarettes.

When the doctor had told George to stop smoking after his bleeding ulcer, I had tried hard to make George follow my example in giving up. He had been to hypnotists, and I had bought him doodling pads for the car. I had also bullied, threatened and pleaded with him. But George chose to ignore COPD and continued to smoke.

During 2002 George and John Chilton, the leader of

George's band, decided to stop touring. They were not only tired of touring, they were tired of each other – not surprising after nearly thirty years together. But as the last season at Ronnie Scott's loomed nearer, George began to regret his decision. He didn't relish sitting at home with the Wing Co. and less money. He could still lecture and write books and articles, but he would miss the intoxicating applause from an enthusiastic jazz-loving audience. Then his agent Jack Higgins came to the rescue. He managed a band called Digby Fairweather and his Half Dozen and Jack thought that they would be pleased to have George join them. Most of them were quite young and the youngest, Julian, who played sax and clarinet, had long black ringlets and wonderful looks. Apart from Digby they all had cars and were willing to drive George to the various gigs. With the Feet Warmers, John's band, George and John had been at the mercy of British Rail. Digby had a girlfriend, Lisa, who not only drove but could also organise the CD sales and keep accounts.

Without John Chilton, who had always paid the band and done a great deal of band business, a lot of this work was now my job, and I liked it. I was now a director of George's companies – he had two, one for band work and one for writing. It was my responsibility to check the bank accounts (which I did online), pay the band, deal with the faxes and check the diary. Shirley was only there two days a week. A lot could happen on the other five and anyway, after forty-three years with George, I knew what was important and, usually, what he would want to do.

I felt much more comfortable with Digby and his band, and not only because, in Lisa, I had a female ally. When

George first started in 1975 with John Chilton, our marriage had been rather fragile. George often took girlfriends on tour with him and Marilyn, who was his secretary until 1994, had been so efficient that I had no role in the band business. I missed Marilyn, who had gone to work for the Citizens' Advice Bureau, but without her I had become more involved and now with the new band I chose to think I had become indispensable.

In April, their first year together, Jack was getting George and Digby a great many bookings and it was decided that they would make a record. The recording studio was in the country and George was staying in a nearby hotel. One night he got up to pee, slipped on the bathroom floor and cracked his ribs. A wheelchair was hired to transport him from the hotel to the studio and George, so said all the reviews, made the best record of his career, with 'Rocking Chair's Got Me' and 'September Song' being particularly moving.

Ribs take a long time to heal and for several weeks George was in pain. For the first time in his life he became depressed, and when he went to the doctor she decided to send him for general check-ups which included a chest X-ray.

The X-ray showed a shadow on his lung. I wasn't worried, as it seemed most likely that this was caused by bronchitis. He went for a scan and Candy accompanied him to the hospital to hear the result.

They were in a pub when she rang me. 'It's lung cancer,' she said. 'They've offered him an operation as the tumour is quite small. He's refused it as it would mean cancelling gigs. And he doesn't want chemo or radiation as it might make him feel too ill to finish his book.' (He had a contract with

Penguin to write about old age, provisionally entitled *Slowing Down*.) 'Oh yes, and he doesn't want a biopsy which would confirm the diagnosis as he doesn't like needles. He's very cheerful. I'll put him on.'

CHAPTER 41

Ambushed by Grief

The first person I rang was Nell Dunn. I had known her since the 1960s but we had only become close friends when she wrote a book about grandmothers in which Kezzie and I featured. She also had dogs as well as grandchildren and we often walked together taking it in turn to talk about our two obsessions. Her long-term partner, Dan Oestreicher, had recently had his lung removed followed by courses of chemotherapy and radiation treatment. Coincidentally she had also written a play entitled *Cancer Tales* which told the stories of six different people with cancer. While writing this she had done a great deal of research around the subject and her experience – as well as her sympathetic nature – made her the obvious recipient of my phone call.

The next person I rang was Rachel Miller. Rachel and Jonathan still lived in NW1 and although we were no longer neighbours we were still friends. Rachel was retired as a GP but she is involved with a website about people's experience of illness including cancer and she was able to suggest some questions that I could ask George's specialist.

What George had said to Candy was quite true. He was quite adamant, he didn't want any form of treatment. The following week we went to St Mary's in Paddington to a meeting with the specialist, Dr Kon, and a cancer nurse called Siân. They pointed out again that the tumour was small and could probably be removed quite easily. George stayed resolute. They said that radiation would eventually help with the pain and George said he would consider that when the time came. Siân had given Candy a booklet for me entitled *Living with Lung Cancer* and, armed with the information supplied, I was able to ask questions: what sort of a tumour was it, small cell or non-small cell, the latter being less invasive. Without a biopsy they weren't able to tell us.

I sneaked and told Dr Kon that George had started smoking heavily again, hoping that Dr Kon would order him to stop or risk the tumour growing at an increased rate. Dr Kon just nodded and clearly agreed with George that the harm was already done.

George's dream had been to die either on the river bank having just landed a large trout or in the wings while the audience were giving him a standing ovation. This dream was so much a part of George's myth that for him to die in any other way was unimaginable for both of us.

George reacted in character to what amounted to a death sentence. He would drink as much as he liked, he would give up giving up cigarettes and, knowing I could hardly object, he would see Greckel more or less when he wanted to. He became less depressed and looked forward to his busy year on the road with Digby and finishing his book.

Probably my reaction was also typical – I was devastated. I'm often told that I am a control freak and death is outside one's control. My guilt at the lack of love I had shown to my parents when they first suffered and then died of the same illness, lung cancer, came back to haunt me. There had been other deaths: Patrick, of course; grandparents; but friends too: Sonia Orwell, who died the same year as Patrick, then Bruce Chatwin, and then Teddy Millington-Drake. The deaths begin to mount up. Patrick, Sonia, Teddy and Bruce were all young or middle-aged when they died and the effect of each death is cumulative. George at seventy-six was not young, and not even all that healthy, but he had a strong constitution and seemed indestructible. At least that was what I had thought, and at first I couldn't believe that he was going to die.

When George and Candy had rung me from the pub George said, 'I don't want to see any gloomy faces, OK?' I never knew when the grief I felt was going to ambush me. I could be out shopping, walking the dogs, or talking on the phone to a friend and I would be overwhelmed with a well of tears and a sobbing that left me shaking.

A month after the diagnosis I developed a lump in my throat that wouldn't go away. I looked it up on the web and it seemed probable that I had throat cancer. The coincidence of us both having cancer did not seem surprising to me; after all my parents had both died within a month of each other. My GP was kind and, although not dismissive, did suggest that I might just have 'a lump in my throat'.

At the back of the 'Living with Lung Cancer' pamphlet was a list of counsellors and I started to spare my friends and ring a woman in Wales. I told her how I had begun to plan: how we would manage when George became too breathless to do stairs, and then the funeral, the sale of the cottage, the house, the pictures, what would I do with his suits and hats, where would Kezzie and I live, and what would it be like to be living without this person who so often irritated me. The woman in Wales, who listened patiently to the silences and sobs as well as the frantic planning, said that it was what most women did. That it was a cathartic and useful thing to do, a good way of coping and, of course, staying in control.

What also helped me get through the days was walking the dogs. When George had decided against the hearing dog I bought a puppy. Kezzie already had a cat, Ollie, a beautiful Burmillar who was loved by all of us, but we thought his confident and sanguine nature would allow him to accept a stranger in the house. Joey is a Papillon. He is only 'pet

quality' as his ears should have more fringes to them. In the dog books Papillons are described as 'cat-friendly', remaining very playful until they are old. I hadn't realised that this would mean I would have to spend my days on my hands and knees playing tug of war with an old sock in my mouth, so I got a friend for Joey, another Papillon called Bobby, also 'pet quality' because of his overhung jaw. These drawbacks have not prevented me from loving them nearly as much as I loved Tuppy and James Sebastian Fox.

While I walked them I could sometimes walk away from my confused, unhappy feelings. It's very easy to accept sympathy from animals. With friends you feel some responsibility: to get better, not to be a bore, to respond in some way and to reassure them that they have said the right things. With the dogs I could be alone, which I often needed to be, and never feel lonely. When I lay slumped in my room

I found the three warm bodies taking up most of the bed all the comfort that I could cope with. My state of mind was in direct contrast to how George seemed to feel. He was cheerful, high even. Siân the nurse told me that this wasn't unusual, it was often the partner who collapsed.

A few months before George's diagnosis, I had begun to worry about leaving him alone in London if I was away, either at the cottage or on holiday. As well as the danger of his falling, George was inclined to leave keys in the front door, the gas on and the shower running.

The solution came from two friends, Anna Coote and Carmen Callil. Independently they had both read about an organisation called Home Share. Basically Home Share finds au pairs for old people. The person engaged can be either sex but has to like old people and be over twenty-five. No money changes hands, as the person only has to be there at night and do eight hours' light work a week in exchange for their room.

When Desdemona came for her interview we didn't know about the lung cancer; when she moved in, a month later in May 2003, we did. Desdemona comes from Zimbabwe, she has refugee status over here and is doing a fine arts degree. We have been incredibly lucky. She is beautiful, wise and tolerant. Back home she has several dogs, a ten-year-old daughter who lives with her mother, three brothers (two of them living in London), two sisters, one of them being slightly disabled, and Des (as I call her) also nursed a grandmother with dementia. She has no problem in coping with our family.

Three months after his diagnosis, I decided that as

George's next birthday might be his last, we would celebrate it at the cottage and I would organise a week of friends visiting for lunch, dinner or staying. It was August and he was going to be seventy-seven. The weather was sunny, the food (cooked by Deanne, a neighbour and professional cook) was perfect, and Suellen Dainty, one of my best friends, came and polished glasses, made beds and set the table. First came Mark and Lydia, friends from Oz; then Mick Mulligan, George's old band-leader, with his wife, Tessa. The following day Louisa Buck, an old girlfriend, arrived with her little boy. Candy took a week off work to be with us; and Julian Mitchell the playwright and his partner Richard Rosen drove over from Wales. On the last day Polly Devlin and her husband Andy Garnett came.

But it wasn't George's last birthday. A month later we saw the specialist again, George had another X-ray and this time there was no sign of a tumour.

Poor George, who finally owned up to COPD, had to give up smoking all over again.

CHAPTER 42

Don't Fence Me In

B eing allowed to smoke again wasn't the only benefit that George enjoyed while we thought he had lung cancer. He told Desdemona that I was being very kind and patient with him. And I was, and for a while it lasted. I also took over the task of managing his medicines.

As well as his various inhalers, George has pills for psoriasis, heart failure, cholesterol, stomach ulcers and depression. Each day there is a different selection: every Thursday there's one pill which has to be taken standing up and on an empty stomach, on Tuesday there are four little yellow pills – methotrexate for the psoriasis – three times a week another yellow pill – folic acid, to counteract the effect of the methotrexate. Seven other pills are swallowed through-out the day to keep George alive and cheerful. One of the pills makes him pee non-stop for hours and therefore he is reluctant to take it, but when he doesn't his feet and calves swell to alarming proportions.

Before I took charge it wasn't unusual to find pills

scattered all over the floor, and quite often he would run out of something just before a weekend. I bought pill boxes from the chemist with the days of the week along the top and times of the day down the side. Now, there was no longer the worry of Bobby and Joey licking up the scattered pills, and George took his medication properly. When he went on tour he sometimes forgot to take the box. That didn't happen very often because if his feet swelled he couldn't wear his best shoes or his spats and he hated going on stage in trainers.

At Christmas he was singing as usual at Ronnie Scott's. Andrée and Oscar came over from Ibiza to see him. They had thought it would be for the last time, but George had bounced back, he'd put on some of the weight he'd lost, he loved his new band and every morning Digby rang to say that he'd been given a standing ovation.

I stopped being quite so wonderful, and life went back to normal. Every Tuesday I went over to Putney where Tom and Lu lived and took India, my new granddaughter, shopping. There was always a slight tug of war in the shopping centre as I needed groceries, and India, although not yet two, felt she needed yet another frilly skirt from Monsoon. Perhaps she is going to be a Tiller girl like her great great granny.

Every week I went to the pictures with Carmen at our local cinema and every day I walked the dogs. Arabella sometimes borrowed a dog so I had another friend apart from Nell and Carmen to walk with. Kezzie struggled with the revision for her A/S exams. Now seventeen and a half, the age I was when Patrick was born, she is tall with long red hair and beautiful like her mother. George slept a lot when he wasn't singing or lecturing – and then he had another fall.

I was at the cottage when I heard. It was February, only six weeks since his successful season at Ronnie Scott's, and I was optimistically sowing broad beans in my vegetable plot when the phone rang.

'Diggers here, Di,' said the cheerful voice of George's band-leader. 'Nothing to worry about, but the master has had a fall. We took him to hospital, they discharged him and we drove him home to put him to bed. They want him to go to his local hospital later on today.' I asked how it had happened and Digby explained that George had done a wonderful last set, stepped forward to take a bow and fallen off the stage into the auditorium. Before going to hospital he had sat in the foyer signing records.

I rang George and realised that the whisky had worn off and he was now in pain so I rang 999 and arranged for an ambulance to take him to hospital. Then I rang George to tell him to be ready, but this time he didn't answer, so I rang my neighbour who had a key. Thank God she was in and was able to go round and wait with George. I packed up the cottage, checked my leaving list and left for London. When I pulled over at a service station I rang Candy, who said she would go to the hospital and bring him back if he was discharged. He was, but his collar-bone was broken and he was in a lot of pain.

And he was in pain for the next few weeks: he could only sleep sitting up and he wasn't allowed – or able – to fish. The gigs were another matter and he refused to cancel any of them. I can only suppose that the amount of adrenalin that cascaded through his body at the sight of an enthusiastic audience compensated for the pain. On stage he was fine, off stage he wasn't. For the first time in his life he was lonely, cross and grumpy. When we went to the hospital to arrange for his collar-bone to be set they said that his heart and lungs weren't strong and he might not survive an anaesthetic.

'We don't have to do it,' they explained, 'but one shoulder will be higher than the other.'

This prognosis delighted George, who staggered to his feet and did his favourite impersonation of Charles Laughton in *The Hunchback of Notre Dame*.

At home he was drinking too much and watching daytime TV. His favourite programmes were about animals or cleaning the house. 'Did you know', he would say, as I dumped a bowl of soup in front of him, 'that vinegar is the only cleaning aid you need?' 'And a pair of hands,' I snapped back.

It took an 'incident' for George to come to his senses about drinking. One afternoon I found him wandering about the house, unsure of where he was, and trying to make a bed up in the kitchen. He was frightened and seeing things that weren't there. I was afraid he'd had a stroke, but when the doctor examined him later on that evening he explained that it was only a combination of pain-killers and whisky.

With the doctor looking on and with George's agreement, I took the bottles from the table next to where he sat and put them in another room. At least he would have to get up out of his chair for a refill. The following week he'd forgotten that he'd agreed to this arrangement. 'No sex, no cigarettes and now no drink – are you trying to fence me in?'

It's me who's fenced in, I thought.

*

IN JULY, A YEAR after his non-lung cancer, and five months since his fall from the stage, George went fishing for the first time. He didn't catch anything but he was thrilled to be back on the river.

Yet again he has bounced back. Lunches with Venetia and Greckel have been resumed, his date sheet, although interspersed with numerous hospital appointments, is full of gigs and lectures. At last he is getting on with his book, entitled *Slowing Down*, and I suppose he is – but not much. He is often quite maddeningly cheerful, and if possible he is even deafer.

THE OTHER DAY George and I had lunch with my brother. He is twenty years older than Wendy, his wife, and we talked about the advantages for him, and for George, in having a wife young enough to take on a caring role.

'Do you mind?' he asked me when George had gone to the loo.

'No I don't,' I said. 'I owe him.'

'But do you love him?' he said.

I was embarrassed by the question. 'I don't know,' I replied.

When I got home I looked up 'love' in the dictionary. It says 'to have a great attachment to and affection for'. So I could have said, 'Yes, I do.'

It gives another definition, 'in a state of strong emotional and sexual attraction', and there was a time when I could have said yes to that one too.

Acknowledgments

I want to thank the following for all the help they have given me while I was writing this book:

Sally Berriff, Jo Binns, Charlie Boxer, Carmen Callil, Gill Coleridge, Anna Coote, Suellen Dainty, Alan Dawson, Yvette Day, Polly Devlin, Nell Dunn, Peter Eyre, Kate Figes, Christina Fitzpatrick, Poppy Hampson, Patrick Hargadon, Dr Mel Henry, Lucy Luck, Alison Lurie, Sergey Maloletkin, Pandora Melly, Tom Melly, Jane and Karl Miller, Dr Rachel Miller, Julian Mitchell, Desdemona Ndanga, Alannah Orr, Andree Quitak, Alison Samuel, Dr Justin Schlicht, Rebecca Simor, Jo Sonn, Emma Tennant, Candy Upton, Francis Wyndham and the late Anne Wollheim.

CREDITS

The epigraph on p. vi is from *The Complete Works* (essay no. 31), Michel de Montaigne, trans. Donald M. Frame (Everyman's Library, 2003).

I am grateful to the following for use of poems and illustrations in the text: George and Tom Melly for their poems; Dr Ellen Ruth Moerman and the Estate of Jean Rhys for lines from an unpublished poem by Jean Rhys; John Chilton for the additional lyrics from 'Life With You'; George Melly for his drawing of 'Mrs Perfect' on p. 125; Steve Benbow for his photo of George and Kezzie on p. 204; John Stefanidis for the painting by Teddy Millington-Drake on p. 222.

List of Illustrations